LAWPACK

101 WAYS TO GROW YOUR BUSINESS

by Hugh Williams FCA

101 Ways to Grow Your Business
by Hugh Williams FCA

1st edition 2005
2nd edition 2007
3rd edition 2010
4th edition 2012

© 2005, 2007, 2010, 2012 Lawpack Publishing Limited

Lawpack Publishing Limited
76–89 Alscot Road
London SE1 3AW

www.lawpack.co.uk

ISBN: 9781909104051
ebook ISBN: 9781909104075

MIX
Paper from
responsible sources
FSC® C011748

Exclusion of Liability and Disclaimer

Contents

Essentials for your business

Essentials for the longer term

Quick ideas to put into practice

Slightly more time-consuming ideas for putting into practice

Now it's up to you

About the author

Hugh Williams FCA is senior partner of H.M. Williams Chartered Accountants (HMWca), the firm he founded in 1973. He has written a number of bestselling books on tax, law and business.

The firm is recent winner of the prestigious Butterworth Tolley Award for best small to medium UK tax team. It has also won the coveted *Daily Telegraph*/Energis National Customer Service Award in the small professional and business services category. In 2004, it reached the last three in the national Accountancy Age Awards for the UK's best small accountancy practice.

Acknowledgements

It is impossible to thank everyone who has either been involved in this book or who, wittingly or unwittingly, has helped this book come about. But here are the names of those kind people that I remember as this book heads for the printers:

Paul Dunn

Robert Townsend

Rick Payne

Everyone at Results Accountants Systems (now Results Accountants Network)

Chris Fredericksen

Iain Fletcher

Gordon Gilchrist

The late Peter Stafford

The late Wally (I never met him nor knew his surname but his video is unforgettable)

Jamie Ross and everyone at Lawpack

Kevan Kennedy

Jessica Cecil-Wright

Peter Lee

John Mitchell

Ted Johns

Terry Woodger

Everyone in my office:

Tim Smith

Mary Huggins

Jacky O'Donnell

Rachael Holmes

Sharon Calley

Roz Rachman

Pat Joseph

Iain Watson

Debbie Johns

Lisa Sword

All my friends who either work at or are members of the Institute of Chartered Accountants in England and Wales

Others whom I have mentioned in this book and all those whom I have forgotten and who I hope will forgive me!

For Paul Dunn

If you hadn't explained to me quite how vital it is to try to dazzle your clients and customers with first-rate service, we would never have won the awards we have, we would never have found such fulfilment in our work and this book would never have been written. Thank you.

Introduction

In this book you'll find many ways to grow your business. Some of these ways may surprise you but if they do, just stop and think, 'What is it that makes you buy from a particular business?' It isn't a confident salesperson or a particular selling process that's taught in the refined atmosphere of the world's leading business schools. No, it's because what the business does, and the way it does it, suits your needs. It's the way that a business behaves towards you that makes you react favourably and make a purchase. Furthermore, when you think about it, some of your most important needs are the little things that a business does for you, like giving you a cup of proper coffee instead of a mug of instant.

The reason it's the little things that matter is because, very often, it's only these that we see when we do business with a company. And, with only the little things to judge businesses by, as a result, we all tend to think, 'If they are getting the little things right, then the likelihood is that I can trust them to get the whole service right.' So this book is (nearly all of it) about the little things you should be doing for your customers and that is why they will not cost you your life's savings to implement.

To help you get the most from this book I have designed it to be a quick and easy read – a quick 'dip into' sort of book – just like the wonderful book *Up the Organisation* by Robert Townsend. His book was an example of how to write a business book with impact and I am trying to follow his method here. What this means is that you have a choice. You can, if you want, read this through from start to finish, like any other book, or you can dip into it, picking subjects at random, as and when you get a moment to do so.

When you come across an idea that you'd like to develop in your business, do turn to the following two lined pages (the ones headed 'Top priorities' and 'Second priorities') and jot the idea down as appropriate. When you have finished reading this book, you'll have two lists to put into action and the rest will be up to you. Good luck!

Top priorities – ideas to implement now

Second priorities – ideas to implement at a later date

Essentials for you

1 Be prepared for success

You must forgive me if what follows seems egotistical, but I discovered it myself, believe that it's important and therefore want to pass it on to you.

When my company found out that we had won two national awards I began to wonder what on earth we had done (got right) to win them. I mean, I didn't think we were *that* different from the competition, but these two independent panels of judges had been led to believe that we were and had singled us out. But what was it?

I looked through our submissions to try to discover what it was that the judges had liked and it seemed to me that there were ten elements that must have weighed in our favour. I gave each of these elements a descriptive name and then took the initial letters of each to see if I could arrange them into a well-known phrase or saying.

The anagram that fell out in front of me spelled Be Prepared and I would now like to tell you what each of those ten letters stands for. I believe that the following formula can be used in business, private life, sports, the arts or anything. Why not try it:

B stands for BELIEVE

You must thoroughly believe in what you are doing, taking charge and full responsibility. It must be of the utmost importance to you.

E stands for EXAMINATION

What you are doing is going to be examined, assessed and tested by someone. On the basis of this examination, you will pass or fail; the customer will buy or put it back on the shelf, etc. So you must focus intensely on this moment at which the success of your project will be determined.

P stands for PERSEVERANCE

There are unlikely to be any quick fixes. It will be hard graft. Others may well object, laugh at you, snigger or sneer. You must keep focused and keep going.

R stands for RESPECT

You must respect the people and processes involved. If you throw your weight about and upset people, you will not make it easy for them to award you the prize. With respect comes the need to be humble and gentle in your dealings with everyone.

E stands for making it EASY for the judges to give you the prize

You have to imagine yourself as the judge – the person with the power to grant you success or failure. Try to imagine what he would like to see if he is to give you the prize and make sure he gets it.

P stands for PATIENCE

This isn't quite the same as perseverance. It may take many years before you win, so don't be surprised if you have to wait. The wait may involve others saying 'I thought you were going to win at X. What's gone wrong?' Well, they must be patient, just like you.

A stands for ALONE

You will spend a lot of time on your own or in a very small team. Don't expect your progress to be glamorous or full of support from others. You may even find that ultimate success isn't met with applause from those who know you. Don't worry – they are not the judges of your success; it's you. Their views, by that time, will be irrelevant.

R stands for RESEARCH

You must keep researching in order to improve what you have set out to do. This means keeping your antennae switched on all the time to pick up anything, from any direction, that might help you improve your project.

E stands for ENJOYMENT

In all of this you must reap enjoyment as you make progress. If you hate what you are doing, you are unlikely to win any prizes.

D stands for DIFFERENT

If you are to stand out from the crowd, what you do must be different and look different if it's to catch the eye or imagination of the judge or customer.

Now, this list isn't meant to be exhaustive, but it may well be useful for you to assess the work you and your business are currently doing and to test whether you pass each test.

For example:

1. Do you **believe** in what you are doing at work?

2. Do you focus on the **exam** moment when the customer is deciding to buy?

3. Are you **persevering** rather than being in it for the short term?

4. Do you **respect** the whole process, your customers, your employees, your trade or profession, your suppliers, etc.?

5. Do you make it **easy** for customers to buy?

6. Are you **patient**?

7. Do you mind striving **alone**, possibly, even with your friends and competitors ridiculing what you do?

8. Do you **research** what is going on so you are up to date?

9. Do you **enjoy** what you are doing?

10. Is your business **different**? Does it stand out from the rest?

2 Plan to build a business of real worth

It's sad to think that so many businesses are started by people who want to earn a crust and not by people who think, 'One day I'd like to sell my business so that I can retire on the proceeds and do what I want for the rest of my life.' The former attitude results in someone building up a job, not a business.

In my opinion, a business is a place where, if the boss is ill or doesn't turn up for work one day, the work (earning capacity) of that business still continues in his absence. A place of work where everyone and everything relies on the boss being there isn't a business – it's simply a glorified job.

To build a business that has some worth which might be realised one day, one has to delegate, train and empower. Test yourself. Do you go to work each day to do the things that your business does (meet the customers, answer the phones, order the stock)? If so, you simply have a job. But if you go to work to manage the business and the money-earning side is looked after by others in the workplace, then you have a business and it will be of value.

How do you get from one to the other? You have to make a decision and take a plunge. You have to start giving responsible work to your employees, handing over the reins to them and letting them make mistakes. This immediately frees up your time for you to plan the business's future. Focus on that day when you will walk away from it with a cheque (or whatever you want) in your pocket.

But so few people do this. Most end up walking away from their own business with nothing to show for it because they went on doing it, doing it, doing it and never made a plan to create something of real worth.

Have you got a plan?

3 Be polite

In the introduction to this book I mentioned that the little things are the most important. Well, politeness is just such a point. Indeed it's probably the strongest point one could make in this context.

Politeness in the dictionary is described as being 'courteous and well mannered' and then below it the dictionary also defines the word as 'cultured, refined and polished'.

So this doesn't just mean putting up with customers without snarling; it means going out of your way to make them feel better. It means showing a cheerful and genuine smile when you greet them (remember, they may have just had some bad news, or someone may have rubbed them up the wrong way at the newsagents; so your friendly face may mean far more to them than you could ever guess).

It means making time for everyone, thanking people (including thanking customers for their custom or even thanking them for making contact with you in the first place, even if they don't end up doing business with you).

It also means thanking those with whom you work because, if you make them feel better, they will do their best for you and for your customers by extension.

Are you putting this necessary face to the fore in everything your business does? Is your receptionist friendly and caring? Does your telephonist answer the phone in a friendly way? Do the managers and bosses care about their people?

It seems so easy, doesn't it, yet we all get it wrong from time to time. People catch us out and we just drift into an irritating response. We may think it's not been noticed but it will have been. 'What's up with him?' people will say, 'I didn't like that tone of voice.'

However, if we have been guilty of rudeness, we have a wonderful escape route. We have a way of putting things right to such an extent that things end up better than before. All we need do is apologise: say sorry, send flowers, a card or a letter and watch how the person you may have offended immediately says, 'Oh, please don't mention it', possibly adding, 'It was my fault for interrupting you when you were busy.'

Politeness and courtesy have these incredible powers for doing good. Milk them for all they are worth!

4 Learn from other businesses

This is one of the best ways of growing a business. You watch to see what other people are doing and then set about doing it better than them.

Now, please note that you don't have to copy people in your own business sector. They can be imitated but, in my opinion, if you introduce something new to your business that you have seen in a different sector, it's likely that you will be the first to do it in your own. You can then more easily steal a march on the opposition than if you start doing something new that is already being done by a competitor. Let me give you an example from across the Atlantic that might apply to any sort of business:

There's a firm of accountants who, when they go to visit a client, always take a box of Danish pastries and they have their own name in big letters on the outside of the box. They have a baker's shop next door to their offices so it's no big deal for them to make the effort, but it's become quite a hallmark and people like it.

Indeed, I have copied them to a small extent. When I visit clients away from Cornwall I try to take a saffron loaf with me. This loaf is pretty rare outside Cornwall and I'm happy to have achieved a small reputation as the accountant who comes with something different.

Unfortunately, this example may not be relevant to your business, but the principle is that whenever you are buying from someone, whether in a shop, restaurant, hotel, railway station or airport, whether in your own country or overseas, or even when merely reading the newspaper or watching the TV, observe what is happening. Watch to see if the people who are serving their customers are doing something unusual – something you've not seen before and which you like – and then think of ways you can do something similar in your own business.

This works the other way too. For instance, if you see someone doing something badly and you realise that you too are guilty of such behaviour in your own business, decide then and there to stop it.

In short, keep those antennae out at all times to see what others are up to and if it's good, try it in your own business.

5 Don't swear

Of all the things one may have to give up in life, swearing has to be the easiest. I will explain why in a moment, but let's see just how dreadful swearing is. First of all, it can be a great offence in its own right (if swearing has any rights of its own). Secondly, it's everywhere – on the TV, in plays, in books, on our own lips. Thirdly, it's always noticed. If ever a word gets remembered from a sentence, it's the swear word.

Now, I'm not going to preach because I used to be a dreadful swearer throughout my boyhood years until my thirties, but one day I was in a taxi with my very good friend Martin Gwynne. We had to swerve alarmingly to avoid a pedestrian who had shot out in front of us and I let out my usual supply of expletives, whereupon Martin said, 'You must stop that swearing, Hugh.' Whereupon I did immediately and I got out of that taxi no longer a swearer. (Thank you, Martin.)

Then a few years later I was at a football match with my young daughter on my right, and the man on my left was swearing like a trooper. After a while I said to him (luckily, he was supporting Plymouth Argyle, like me) 'Please watch your language, I have my young daughter with me.' 'Oh, sorry, mate,' he replied and never swore again for the rest of the match. I suspect, he too could well have given it up for good.

I can recall two other people, one a client, who used to swear. She was letting fly one day and said, 'Oh, Hugh, I shouldn't do that. You don't swear, do you?' (I was quite unaware that we had ever discussed whether I did or not, but she was right.) I simply said, 'It doesn't become you' and now she has stopped. Now, whether that was because of my tiny comment or not, I don't know.

One of business heroes (who shall also remain nameless) used to swear on stage enormously. He mentioned how proud his mother was of him but 'she doesn't like my swearing'. I said to him on one occasion, 'Your mother's right' and the next time I heard him, you have guessed it, not a swear word was heard. Again, I won't take any credit. I'm simply pointing out how easy it is to stop swearing.

Clients, on the whole, will hate it if you swear. As we have seen, it's very easy to stop.

6 Go the extra mile

You should always try to think of everything when it comes to looking after your customers.

If you think about it, most businesses perform just like their competitors. Now, is your customer care the same as your rivals? What makes your service any different from theirs? The danger (inevitably) is that there may be nothing to distinguish your business from your competitors' in the eyes of your customers.

So how do you inject a difference? The answer is that you inject that ingredient called 'going the extra mile'.

How you do this isn't easy to advise. It has to be something that you want to do. You could ask your customers what extra service they would like to see you do or you may be able to work it out on the basis of identifying what extra products or services you could provide. You may be able to work it out from the following true anecdote:

This is a true story about three top garages and a top industrialist and it illustrates, beautifully, how important it is to get little things right in the running of a business.

The top industrialist wanted to change his car and he first of all went to Garage A. He found a suitable car and the garage said that it would get back to him with a trade-in price on his old car. As far as we know, he still hasn't heard back from it.

The next garage he approached was Garage B and the salesman, who told us the story, said that he took the car to be tested, which was full of petrol, out to the industrialist's home so that he could try it for a day. The salesman then took the car to be traded-in back to his garage and when he returned it, not only had the old car been valeted but it too had a full tank of petrol.

The next garage to be approached was Garage C. The industrialist drove the car away on a trial run. Within three miles, the petrol light came on and when, a few miles later, he turned the car to go back to the garage, the windscreen washer light also came on.

At this point, the industrialist said to himself, 'I can't be doing with all this inefficiency from Garages A and C. I'm definitely going to buy the car from Garage B as it knows how to look after me.'

The point of this story is that the decision to purchase was not made on the quality of the car, the price of the car, the length of time it took to deliver – it was made on the quality of service which shone from one garage and was either non-existent, or apparently non-existent, from the others.

In short, it's the little things that we, in business, have to get right and this is what growing a business is all about.

Could attention to detail in that sort of way work for you?

7 Use a mentor

When I first wrote this point, I entitled it, 'Even Olympic Gold medallists need coaches'. In other words, while you may be the best person in the whole wide world at what you do, you should still employ the services of a mentor or coach. Why?

The first reason is that a mentor keeps you honest. The way it works is that if you make a plan to do some important new things in your business but only tell yourself that this is in your plan, the chances are you will do nothing and let yourself and the business down. If you are the only person you report to, it's so easy to drop the idea because you couldn't be bothered or something else cropped up. If, on the other hand, you have told an independent mentor what you plan to do, he will come along once in a while and say, 'How are you getting on?' and if you have done nothing, you will have let him down as well as yourself, and you will be embarrassed at your failure. This whole scenario of using a mentor is a trigger for making things happen.

Secondly, a mentor will probably be impartial. If your ideas are daft, he will almost certainly tell you. Then, if your ideas need a tweak or two, he will also tell you and may be able to offer ideas that solve any shortcomings.

Thirdly, a mentor is someone with whom you will find disasters are halved and successes doubled. This is so important. I always think that if I were good at tennis (and I'm useless), I would prefer to win the Wimbledon men's doubles title than the singles. If I won the singles, after a while of saying 'Wasn't that terrific?' my wife would say, 'Oh, do stop going on about it. Yes, you won it but there are other things in life. Can't you move on?' and I'd begin to mope that my winning wasn't appreciated. But if I had won the doubles, I could go to my playing partner and say, 'Wasn't that great!' and neither he nor I would ever bore each other by talking of the victory.

It's the same in business. If you have no business partner or mentor, you may have nobody you can share successes with. Life, even successful business life, can be lonely. However, with a mentor, you have someone on whose shoulders to cry if necessary and someone with whom you can open a bottle (or two) of champagne when things go really well.

So try to appoint a mentor (he needn't be a business expert – just someone you like and trust) and see how that very simple addition can make profound things happen.

8 Remember the second commandment

While this is a business book and in no way does it set out to be a religious tome, the second commandment makes brilliant sense when it comes to doing business. What it says is 'Love thy neighbour as thyself', but some paraphrase this commandment as 'do as you would be done by'.

When relating this commandment to business, we should think of how we like being treated and then start treating people the same way.

After following this commandment, the first thing one notices is how much nicer business becomes. However, I'm not suggesting that you turn yourself into someone who makes life a drudgery and become a dogsbody. No, I mean it's a way of doing business that sheds light and happiness and fun into not just your workplace, but to everyone with whom you come in contact.

In many ways, this whole book centres on this point. It's the only point one really needs to read because, from this philosophy, all the other ideas develop. Indeed, they rely on this concept.

9 Go with your hunches – take risks

So often we do things in life because everyone else has done them or it's a safe option. But you will see that taking that line in life is a cop out; it's the easy option.

Yet we all do it. Indeed, while my life has been full of wonderful things, I fully accept that for so much of it, I have been guilty of simply doing what other people have suggested, rather than going with my own hunches. It's those who go with their hunches that make the breakthroughs; those who follow in the footsteps of others often don't.

My heroes who broke the mould include St Thomas More, Beethoven, John Constable and Kelly Holmes (I don't mean to imply equal weight to them all, by the way), but, if these four had only done what others suggested, instead of following their own hunches, we would never have heard of them and others would now be filling their places.

So if you are good at music, or athletics, or something else and you enjoy doing it, please have a go. Others may scoff. It will, not just may, be hard, and you may fail, but you will always be able to look yourself in the eye and say, 'At least I tried'.

This is the same in business. If you have an idea that might be the real McCoy and if you have lived with it for a long time, you simply *have* to give it a go. It might be a product or it might just be some sort of customer service wheeze that you believe could be terrific. Please go with it. The chances are that you will be right.

10 Don't be the cheapest – be the best

I know this is obvious, but we all tend to forget to think this through and take appropriate action.

It has been said, and rightly, that your competitors will never put your own prices up – only you will ever do so and let's face it, how often are you brave enough to do it?

If your prices are (as they should be) moving up, but you are not doing anything to command higher prices, your customers will not like the increase and will take their custom elsewhere.

But if your prices are going up and, at the same time, you are reminding your customers that they should come to you because you are the best in town, then they will tend to stick with you. We all like to be associated with success stories and once you start using a product or service that is renowned for being a market leader, you don't tend to put up with a second-rate alternative.

So to achieve this, you must consider yourself to be the best, try to attain it and charge a price to match this image!

11 Don't FTI

Those of you who have seen a very inspiring video about a man called Wally (and I have never quite got Wally's surname) will know what FTI stands for. It stands for 'fail to implement'.

Wally's message (sadly, Wally died a few days after this famous video was filmed) was that we all have great ideas, but if we don't do anything with them, nothing will happen; implementation, not inspiration, is the problem. So FTI disease is a scourge of all humanity.

How does one fight this disease, especially in our businesses? I think the best way is to get an independent mentor to work with you – see point 7.

Another way is simply to go public and say to your employees, 'I'm going to try to do XYZ' and then you will know that others will spot it if you fail even to start.

A third way is to share not just the ideas, but also their implementation with your employees. If, as a team, you say, 'Right. Enough is enough. We're going to crack this one and succeed', the chances are that something will happen.

But if it stays in your head, it stays in your head.

12 My Savoy dream

May I indulge a little?

In 1994 my wife, Alice, and I celebrated 20 years of marriage and I decided to take her to the Savoy Hotel in London. Both her parents and mine had stayed there; my in-laws even married in The Savoy Chapel during the Second World War. I made all the bookings and set off from Surrey with the aim of reaching the hotel shortly after noon, comfortably in time for lunch.

But the London traffic was dreadful and held us up for an hour or more and we were very late arriving. Now, this delay annoyed me greatly – our special time together was going wrong from the very beginning, so we eventually drove into the Savoy forecourt, very late and pretty upset. But as I brought the car to a halt, three people came out to meet us: one to welcome us and escort us to the reception desk, another to collect our luggage from the boot and the third to drive the car away and park it for us. As we walked in through the revolving doors, a tide of care seemed to embrace and overwhelm us. The Savoy took away all my angst and we just loved the care the hotel lavished on us.

When we left two days later, after 48 hours of such cosseting, I found myself saying, 'I want our accountancy practice to be to our profession what the Savoy is to the hotel industry.' We felt cared for throughout our visit – yes, we had paid for the care, but we had really got value for money. I now wanted to copy that care in the way we at our firm treated our clients.

My dream helps me emphasise how, if we aim to be the best, we have to do something to be the best. And if we can reach the heights that the Savoy has reached, the world will not just come to us in numbers, but everyone will look on us from afar as being the place to do business with – the place by which (the standard against which) all others are judged.

To find that within eight years of creating this dream, we had won two national awards makes me feel that we have climbed up a few rungs towards fulfilling that initial dream, but it all started with a dream.

Why not try to fulfil your dreams too?

13 Don't be pompous

I know this is an obvious thing to say but, particularly among professionals, there is a tendency to be superior in how we talk to our clients. Those who are pompous think they impress their clients. They think it makes them look frightfully superior as they live in the mystique of very complicated technical stuff.

Wrong! Pomposity puts the customer off. You get far more business if you sit down and explain to your customers, in everyday language, what's going on. What you do and what it means to them.

14 Go on until you are stopped

This was the maxim that my mother brought me up on. She had been brought up on it by her mother and one wonders how far back one has to go to find the true origin of it.

We all tend to think when pondering a new course of action, 'Ooh, I'd better not do that. It might be wrong. What will other people think?' If we do adopt this approach, we'll soon find that our fears take the upper hand.

On the other hand, if you say, 'I think I'll try doing this thing a different way', the chances are that our hunch will have been right. If they are ill-founded, then the venture will come to an end and we'll have to start again but, more often than not, we will find that we were right after all.

In other words, if we're on the wrong track, the equivalent of the man in the peak cap at the barrier will appear and say, 'Sorry. You can't come through this way' and he'll stop you. But, until he does appear, just keep on going. Go on until you are stopped.

15 Don't be scared of success

My son, Paddy, will cringe at me including this tale about him but it has a good ending and I think his example is an inspiration for all of us.

Paddy is our only son and we have four daughters. Paddy was the fourth to be born, so he has three elder sisters. For part of our married life, my wife and I taught our children at home on our small farm nearly 1,000 feet up in Dartmoor National Park. This meant that, until Paddy was about ten, he didn't have very much male company.

In an effort to put this right, Alice and I decided to hold a sports day for both our and other local children that we knew were being taught at home. We must have had about 20 children come to the event.

Paddy was in the 60-yard dash for the under fives and, you have to realise, he had never beaten anyone in a race before. He'd beat his sisters hollow now with his long legs but, until this home school sports day, he'd always been outrun by his elder siblings.

The race started and, to his amazement, Paddy shot out into the lead. As his father I was thrilled for him but this thrill turned to dismay when Paddy, realising that he was in a totally unfamiliar situation, froze in concerned astonishment. He'd never been in front before. He didn't know what the rules of leading were, especially in front of a crowd of grown-ups all watching and cheering.

Maybe as host of the event I shouldn't have done this but I couldn't resist shouting, 'Go on, Paddy. Go on!' Bless him, this is exactly what he did and he won comfortably.

Now, we often find ourselves in a similar situation to Paddy. We find that we're doing something no-one else seems to be doing.

But we also tend to freeze when we find our efforts being gazed upon. We forget that we set out with the best of intentions and indeed with very clear intentions. So what happens is that, when these intentions are being fulfilled, if anyone else happens to be looking and, worse, passing ill-informed comments, we think we must be wrong and our instinct is to go back and hide in the bushes somewhere.

But it's at this very point in time that we must whip our 'get up and go' into action and see the race through to its successful conclusion.

For heaven's sake, never be scared of success!

16 Just do it!

So often one hears the expression 'Oh, I could never do that!' It's a self-fulfilling prophesy. I do it over bungee jumping. I could never do it. I shudder at the thought of standing up there waiting to be told to jump, or do they push you? (I ought to ask my daughter, Martha, because she's done it; though where she gets it from defeats me). No, I never want to do that; the result is that I will be making no plans whatsoever to do it. See what I mean about self-fulfilling?

On the other hand, think of this: while I come from an independent conservative background, I've always thought that the two MPs I would most like to meet were the left-wingers Michael Foot and Tony Benn. They are extremely well-informed and interesting characters. If you offered me the opportunity of being the third person at a dinner party with those two, I'd jump at it.

So for years I have dreamed of meeting them and, at least, shaking their hands. I made no great plan to do so but the dream was always there. I, as it were, willed the meetings to happen. Lo and behold, they did! A few years ago and with the space of a few months, I met Tony Benn after one of his evening audiences in Exeter and I went up to Michael Foot at Home Park, the home of Plymouth Argyle.

These meetings were far from being earth-shattering events and you, dear reader, may be unimpressed or in total disagreement with my choice of celebrities; but that's not the point. The purpose of the example is that if we want to do something, even if we only vaguely want to do it, there is far more chance of us doing it than if we simply assume that 'it' (whatever that is) will never happen.

So, think of the things you do want to do and start sketching plans for their fulfilment. Write it down (it's best to get a spiral-bound notebook for this sort of vague planning than using the back of an envelope – the book is less likely to be thrown away), visit your musings from time to time and you'll find that things gradually fall into place.

I remember looking at the convertible (soft top) car Volvo produced in early 2000. 'I'd love to have one of those', I thought. I considered them to be the most beautifully designed production car ever manufactured. I kept dreaming about these cars and, yes, you've guessed it. Within 18 months I was the proud owner of one.

So, as around-the-world walker Ffyona Campbell said, you have to live your dreams. If you do, they have every chance of coming true.

17 Time spent on reconnaissance is seldom wasted

This particular lesson might be equally encapsulated as reading 'Don't be afraid of wasting time contacting famous people who might be able to help or encourage you'.

One of the exciting things about business development is that things happen all the time in this area. Take the latest venture I have indulged in

– publishing. Now, the nature of the business need not detain us, but during this last year I have heard about a very rich man who has made his money both in Britain and the USA. If I say he's worth hundreds of millions of pounds that will spare his blushes and yet you will realise that when I say 'very rich' I mean 'very, very rich'.

When my first book was rolling off the press and I was sending out copies for review I decided to send this man a copy – to see if he approved of the philosophy it espoused. I didn't expect to hear from him – not at all. It was a one in a 100 chance he'd even get my complimentary copy.

Imagine my delight one Sunday (yes, Sunday) morning when the phone went and it was him. He'd got my book, he'd read it and he agreed very much with its philosophy and his good wishes were a great confidence booster for me.

In case you are interested the topic where we concurred it concerns the maxim in which I believe so fundamentally of 'never charge by the hour'. He related a ghastly tale of a firm of solicitors who'd got this philosophy so wrong and it's worth repeating here. A few years ago a firm of solicitors had sent him an invoice with the time records pinned to the back. He found himself skimming the details and saw an entry 'Three minutes - to send the managing director our condolences on the death of his father'.

He was speechless; I was speechless when he told me and I'm sure you are speechless right now!

Anyway, I digress. The point is that if I hadn't written to this great man, I would never have received his encouraging pat on the back.

Essentials for your business

18 Employ happy people

Your employees are the people your customers meet. So if you employ happy, friendly people with engaging smiles, not only will this please your customers but it will attract new friendly customers to come and do business with you.

The great explorer Sir Earnest Shackleton employed happy, friendly people and my hunch is that their outlook on life was one of the key reasons why, on his extraordinarily dangerous, and famous, boat journey – an unplanned journey forced on him by the break-up of his ship – he didn't lose a single man.

19 Don't do it on the cheap

I learnt this lesson to my cost with my car. I normally get it serviced in a smart (and yes, expensive) garage just down the road from my office. On one occasion I decided to get the servicing done in another garage – this time in a back street.

I thought that their friendly faces meant that they would do just as good a job as the smart one. How wrong I was. Here is my tale of woe:

The smart one	The cheap one
They always kept me informed as to how my car's servicing was going and when the car was going to be ready	The just waited for me to turn up when I imagined the car would be ready

They always asked if there was anything, apart from the service, that needed doing	There was no chat at the outset and they just said 'thanks 'when I handed over the keys
They always cleaned the car inside and out	They had no complimentary cleaning service
They had a special area where they would look after me – an area for customers	When I called to collect the car, I had to fight my way through the workshop to the office with girlie calendars exposing not just the usual fare but, more importantly, the state of the minds of both the workers and the bosses there
They filled in the service record that lives in the car	They never filled in the service record
They still have my custom	They will not service my car again

But my story doesn't quite end there. A few years later I had a fault with my car and it was out of warranty. It was a part that shouldn't have failed and the smart garage offered to pay for it themselves. But when they sent the paperwork up to head office for their confirmation, because I had had one service at another garage, the amount they were prepared to pay was just 25 per cent of the bill. It never pays to go for the cheaper option!

It will, therefore, always pay you to provide the quality service and all the things I've listed above are little things that cost next to nothing to provide.

20 Reputations are important

One way to create a great reputation is to take note of what others do wrong to you and vow never to do that to your customers.

This is a story from my friend Ted Johns, the Chairman of the Institute for Customer Service.

I won't mention the store but it's a famous one and you've probably visited it. Ted tried to return a product to the Y chain; not because he didn't like the item, but because it was faulty. He complained to Trading Standards about the situation where it took him one and a half hours to get his money back from the store for a £150 faulty phone system. In response, Trading Standards said to Ted, 'Well, you know where you went wrong, don't you? You went in there. You won't catch one of us shopping there.' This was Trading Standards' view of that chain!

The message of this sort of anecdote is as follows:

- Reputations take a long time to win but can be lost in a trice.

- Customers are crying out for shops they can trust, receptionists that empathise and banks that listen.

- Organisations must learn to say sorry sooner.

- High performance, world-class customer service isn't the sole preserve of First Direct, Banyan Tree Hotels, Amazon, John Lewis and Pizza Express.

21 Be sensitive to the personal needs of your employees

If an employee has a problem, such as a difficulty at home, give him the space to sort it out. If you treat him as you would like to be treated if you were suffering from the same thing, you have no idea how much loyalty it will generate and this will lead to the employee respecting your philosophy and continuing to practise great service for your customers.

22 Guarantees

The purpose of guarantees is often overlooked or misunderstood. When, in our accountancy firm, I mentioned to our first customer that if she wasn't happy with the service our staff provided, she was not under any obligation to pay us a bean, she was amazed. 'Wow,' she said, 'you must feel really confident about the quality of your service.'

Funnily enough, it was rather us accepting a cold dose of reality. If we had let this lady down and provided her with a truly lousy service (and all of us can find that we screw up from time to time) and she had no intention of paying us, and we ended up in court and lost, we would not get paid. And even if we had ended up in court and won but she still refused to pay, we still would not have got paid.

So the reality is, if we (and I'm including you in this sentence) produce something for which our customer refuses to pay, we're very unlikely to get paid.

So why not come out with this reality upfront and say at the first meeting, 'If you don't feel that you have received what you consider to be value for money, we don't expect to get paid – and you are the only judge in this matter.' It's a very powerful guarantee, yet it's simply reflecting reality.

The beauty is that nobody ever does this, so this promise really stands out. It has won our small accountancy firm two national awards – our guarantee (which says just this) blew all the other finalists' submissions away and the award panel said that we were clear winners.

Guarantees cost so very little to implement. Very seldom are you taken for a ride and when you are, you don't do business with that person again. Yet guarantees are the things which, if properly publicised, give strangers the confidence to approach you and want to buy from you. Such assurance makes them believe that you will care more about serving them than filling your pockets.

It's no good saying that 'our products are guaranteed' because everyone says this and it means nothing. No, you should think about providing a number of specific guarantees, such as:

- if we don't show up within a half hour of an agreed time, you won't have to pay; or

- if you find that you don't like our product, bring it back within a month and you'll get a full no-quibble refund.

Think of an amazing guarantee and then see how well it goes down.

23 Put the price up (part 1)

This is the bit we all hate doing. We say, 'But I can't do that. Our customers would never wear it. They'd go elsewhere.' If this is your attitude, then you are wrong.

So often I have advised clients to put their prices up by over 20 per cent and it's made all the difference to their businesses and indeed their lives.

The truth is that you have far more of a problem with your price than your customers ever do. What they look for isn't price but value for money. Well, some buy purely on price and if you are in that market, all well and good. But for most businesses, customers buy on value for money, service and convenience.

Let me tell you what happened when we put the price of one of our services up by 25 per cent. This added about £20,000 to our turnover. We lost about ten clients, but the ones we lost were the ones we didn't like anyway and they were small fry (their business accounted for no more than £2,000). So was it worth adding £18,000 to our bottom line and losing a number of unpopular customers at the same time? You bet it was.

Now, your competitors will never put your prices up. It's you that has to make the decision; so just go ahead and do it.

One way to do it is to introduce some new wonderful guarantee at the same time and possibly add in more than one. Make the guarantee so outrageous that its impressiveness completely dwarfs the fact that the price is going up.

However, if you are still worried that you'll lose too many customers, just look at the following chart and see, if you were to put your prices up by a certain percentage, how many customers you could afford to lose before you lose out. You will see that our experience is no freak occurrence.

If your present margin is...								
20%	**25%**	**30%**	**35%**	**40%**	**45%**	**50%**	**55%**	**60%**
Your sales would have to fall by the following percentage before your profits decline...								

And you increase your price by...									
2%	9	7	6	5	5	4	4	4	3
4%	17	14	12	10	9	8	7	7	7
6%	23	19	17	15	13	12	11	10	9
8%	29	24	21	19	17	15	14	13	12
10%	33	29	25	22	20	18	17	15	14
12%	38	32	29	26	23	21	19	18	17
14%	41	36	32	29	26	24	22	20	19
16%	44	39	35	31	29	26	24	23	21
18%	47	42	38	34	31	29	26	25	23
20%	50	44	40	36	33	31	29	27	25
25%	56	50	45	42	38	36	33	31	29
30%	60	55	50	46	43	40	38	35	33

24 Free audits

The word 'audit' is more of an American term than a description of an accountant auditing books. It means doing a survey of your prospective customers' needs, presenting them with a report and not charging them for the work.

Most suppliers say 'free estimates' but that's just boring – everyone does it. Instead, if you are a carpet cleaner, for example, you could offer to visit someone's home and carry out a free survey of:

- the state of the cleanliness of his carpets;

- the mites that are in them; and

- their state of repair.

You will then provide him with:

- a properly presented bound report; plus

- an estimate of what the remedial work will cost; and

- details of all your guarantees.

Such an approach is seen to be caring, professional, helpful and valuable.

It will mean that, if he sees that this is how you approach your prospective customers and compares this approach with what your rivals are doing, you are extremely likely to be called to provide the estimate.

Why not look at your rivals' adverts in the *Yellow Pages* and see what they offer. It's unlikely to be a patch on what is being suggested. I have just looked at the carpet cleaning section in our local *Yellow Pages* and I couldn't see one that was offering a carpet audit.

This isn't rubbishing the advertisements I have just seen. Carpet cleaners probably have the best *Yellow Pages* advertisements there are – these people are very hot on providing valuable guarantees and they know their stuff about customer care. But, to get the customers' attention in the face of this impressive opposition, you have to show more than caring – you have to seem to shout, 'Hey, you, yes, you, the person who wants his carpets cleaned, don't pick up the phone to the first advertiser you see – don't part with your money, or think of doing so, until we have provided you with a free report. Then, once you know what needs to be done, pick whoever you want to do it. We hope it'll be us, but if it is, we want to have earned your business, not sold it to you purely on the basis of some flashy ad.'

Could you provide a free audit for your customers?

25 Free offers

When you see most adverts, you pass over them quickly. We don't tend to buy a newspaper to read the advertisements; our interest is likely to be on the front page, some general news, the letters page, the sports pages and perhaps the crossword. We might have bought the paper to look at the classified advertisement page, but we're highly unlikely to spend time looking at the advertisements.

The reason we treat such advertisements with disdain is because we're saying to ourselves, 'What's in it for me?' We usually have no interest in buying a car, a new TV or booking a holiday – we simply want some peace and quiet in which to read the newspaper and, frankly, the advertisements get in the way.

But if we have seen an advertisement with a free offer (something of value), then we might just spend some time thinking about it. Such offers are potentially much more interesting than just sales pitches.

You could offer a free:

- consumer awareness guide;

- non-committal first meeting;

- phone call (a freephone number);

- postage service (Freepost is an excellent way of helping customers do business with you).

If you can't think of anything free to offer then either:

- look at what your rivals are offering in the *Yellow Pages* – you are bound to spot something there which you could crib; or

- hold a customer advisory board (see point 93). Call in about ten customers and when asking them 'How can we look after you better?', add 'Is there anything we could supply for free?' They are bound to come up with ideas.

Make sure that you offer them something free and you'll notice that your rate of converting prospects into sales improves immeasurably.

26 Systematise

I apologise if this sounds boring, but within this word lies the secret of just about everything anyone may want from a business. The way this works is as follows:

When you think about it, just about everything you do in your business is repetitive. While this principle may not apply to a brain surgeon's job (although I suspect it does), most of the work we do today is the same as what we did yesterday.

If this is the case, it probably doesn't have to be us who always have to do those tasks. If we were being watched by someone yesterday doing what we did, it may not take that person too long to work out what it is that we do and he could start doing it for us. Indeed, in the case of most businesses, if the owner is ill (and so long as there is more than just the owner working in the business), the business tends to carry on without him, and it sometimes carries on much better without him!

If, therefore, you were to take a long hard look at what it is that you do each day (perhaps listing everything down in some detail – how you do it, etc.), it should be possible to get someone else to start doing some of what you do. Wouldn't this free up your time, providing you with the opportunity to take a better look at your business, where it's going and when it might become something of real value?

But, if you are to escape some of your (probably self-made) rat-race, you do have to effect this change deliberately.

I'll come to the golden rules in a moment, but first of all let's just look at what I'm envisaging in action. You may or may not like the example I give but it's the principle I'm espousing here, not the particular. If you were to go into a Kentucky Fried Chicken in this country or one in a different country, you know pretty well, before you enter the place, what it's going to look like. Why is this? Because they are all built around systems. They have systems and the employees are trained how to use and sometimes help contribute to the development of their systems.

So if you want to emulate them and develop systems in your own business, here are the golden rules:

- List in some detail what you do – all those things you would like to get someone else to do for you. This process will be your system.

- Get someone from your organisation (or hire someone fresh) and train them to do this stuff for you. This will show you just how easy it is to manage a business that runs on systems.

- Watch how much the person you hand the process over to enjoys it and how he starts to develop the system into something better than it was before.

27 Delegate

This follows on directly from the previous point. If you have systems that others can follow, use and help to run your business, then you must delegate this work to them.

To some people 'delegating' is a dirty word. It sounds like getting rid of the work you don't want to do: palming it off to some poor soul who cannot refuse to do it. I hope, by the time you have finished this short point, that you will see that proper delegating is a valuable tool in your business growth armoury.

The first point about delegating is that you have to do it. The saying goes that if you can free up your time by (probably) 80 per cent, you will have created a huge reservoir of time for you to plan and manage your business.

The second point is, and this may surprise you, that if you pass on some of your responsibilities to someone working with you, he is far more likely to get excited by the opportunity this affords him than being brassed off by having more work to do. Employees love to excel and, when it comes to giving them new jobs, work and responsibilities, they are likely to relish what you give them, rather than resent it.

If you give them the job to do, then give them the tools of the job as well. Give them free rein to do it and say, 'This system is the one I have been using. If you can think of a better one, let me know and, chances are, I'll give you the wherewithal to try out your ideas.'

So, having got this far, you will find that, in a short space of time, they could easily be doing the job better than you were. None of us can assume that our method is the best or the only method there is. After all, two heads are often better than one, and the very act of delegating could well spark a whole new method of working and an improvement to the bottom line.

With delegating comes the need to train and this means that time and money must be invested in making sure the person understands what it is that he should be doing. He may even need to go on a course or get an extra qualification. But by investing in your people, you will find that they reward you with better work, better systems, a happier workforce and better profits. Not a bad deal, eh?

28 Trust your employees

There is a tendency for some business owners not to trust their employees. Such proprietors tend to regard their workers with suspicion (I suspect they regard everyone, not just their employees, with suspicion); they may think that these people are after their wage packet on the cheap and are in the business of diddling the firm and its owners through their expense claims. Along with this scenario, such employers are always checking up on and criticising the work that's been done and, as a result, there is a disconsolate atmosphere around everyone, with nobody trusting anyone else. This is sad and if you find you are working in such a place, I suggest you find another employer.

I would like to start from a completely different viewpoint and repeat the little-known but nonetheless penetrating slogan that reads 'people love to excel'. We all love doing well. When we win a race at our school sports day, when we got good marks in class, even if our football team does well, we love the pleasure that goes with success and this good effect that success brings is one that, I believe, should be encouraged throughout all places of work.

This is one of the reasons why I think going in for awards is important. Even if you don't go very far the first time you enter, you will learn from the experience and, as time goes by, you will find that your business rises in the pecking order – and this is good for everyone's morale. Chances are, you will win something (some recognition) in due course and have a trophy or prize-winning photograph to hang in your reception. Believe me, customers do notice and appreciate evidence that you are better than the rest.

What does trusting your employees consist of?

- First of all, you must like and respect them. If you don't do so, then there is a problem and I'm not sure what I'd suggest, except that you should try harder!

- You must give them responsible work to do and give them free rein to do it. They will need training, but couple the training with the invitation to review what they find as they do the job and tell them that if it seems to them that there's a better way, you would like to hear their ideas. Please don't appear to be checking up and criticising their work all the time. 'Oh no, you've got it all wrong. I'll do it myself if you can't do it' is a terrible thing to say and a terrible conclusion if that is what they discover you are thinking after you have taken the work back.

- Review their work and thank them for what they have done. Talk to them about it, show them why this new work is important to the success of the business, ask them how they feel it went, if they are happy to be doing it and then consider if there is anything else they might take on.

And the benefits of this process are twofold. Not only are they happier, but also you will find that you are able to do other things with the time you now have available.

29 Make your customers laugh

I'm glad that I fell upon this one. If I hadn't stumbled across it, I probably wouldn't have believed it.

At my company we send our newsletter to our clients. We used to share the costs of doing so with some fellow firms and it went down well but, one day, we decided that we wanted to do our own thing. This way we could control what went into the newsletter; we could personalise it and make it reflect our own philosophy.

The bits that we put into our own newsletter that made all the difference were the jokes. And if you think about this, it makes sense.

Be honest, if you pick up a newspaper, while you will want to read the bits you always read, don't you always look at the cartoons as you leaf your way through? We all do it and those whose job it is to market their business products should take a serious note of this reflection on human nature.

However, most people don't dream of doing this. For example, most professional firms send out boring, turgid newsletters describing the latest news in tax, the law or details of other technical issues. But our clients are just *not* interested in this sort of stuff. This is the reason why they engage professionals to deal with this side of things so that they don't have to get involved. (You may have a few clients who are interested in the boffin-type articles, but they are a small minority, so if you want to impress them, single them out and send them a letter with the clever stuff incorporated into it. By doing this, you avoid boring the masses.)

So be light-hearted. Show that you are human. Let your customers know that although you do a serious job of work, you do have a sense of humour. We keep a book of jokes in our reception for clients to read and it's the book they read the most!

However, the jokes must not be lewd and if they are poking fun at anyone, they should be ridiculing your own profession and not another one – so you can't be accused of taking unfair potshots at others.

For my part, I tend to put things into our newsletter that I come across between editions and which amuse me. If I have giggled at something, the chances are my clients will also enjoy the laugh. Why not buy some cartoons and hang them in reception? You'll be delighted at how much visitors remark on them.

30 Take one day off during your working week

This may seem a perverse suggestion but it's incredibly important. This is because we all seem to be so busy that our very busyness prevents us from taking time off and planning for the future. This lack of time to make a plan can all be changed if you know that one day in the week – and make it fixed every week, say Tuesdays – you will be free from the day-to-day stuff and can think about where you and your business is heading.

Can't be done, you say? Let me tell you how I got started:

In 2000, I told my staff that from 1 September I would no longer work Fridays in the office. From then on, it would be a day I'd spend at home. I would keep a Friday book and, as the week went by, I would list those things that I would do on the following Friday.

Now, to be on the safe side, I said that this idea would be an experiment until Christmas. That way, if it didn't work out (if my clients found that they could never get hold of me, etc.), I could return to a five-day week with no loss of faith. However, it worked a treat.

Firstly, my clients were impressed. This may be the reverse of what you would expect, but this move reflected well, rather than badly, on my business reputation. In fact, a number were rather envious of this plan and a couple actually copied me.

Secondly, it went down well with my employees. They had one day a week when I wasn't breathing down their necks and they liked it.

Thirdly, my body liked it. I could get up when I wanted on a Friday. Fridays could be used for haircuts, trips to the dentist, playing golf with my son at half-term and generally being more available to help my hard-working wife with her chores.

But, fourthly, the business benefited as I could plan ahead. Some of my Fridays were spent on work (yes, I did take some work home), but were it not for the Fridays, I would never have written our bestselling book *Tax Answers at a Glance* and this very title and I would never have had the time to enter for three national awards.

Do give it a go. It makes work and play much more fun and rewarding when you have a day that is divided between the two as you see fit – a day that belongs to you.

31 You never know where your next customer will come from

I have to tell you a story here – one against the author!

Some years ago, the front door to the office opened and in came a man wanting to sell us a burglar alarm. He had made an appointment, but I had forgotten about it and when my secretary told me he had arrived, I let out an audible moan (one this man must have heard) as if to say, 'Oh no, I hate being interrupted. Why can't people leave me alone to get on with what I have to do?'

Well, I had to see him and so I did. Now, remember, he had come to sell me a burglar alarm which I didn't want, but when he first phoned to make the appointment I thought that he might encourage me to use one. However, I didn't buy a burglar alarm. What happened was that 45 minutes later he left my office as a client of mine.

Now, did I deserve him to become a customer of mine? Not at all, if you think of the grudging way I approached meeting him in reception. But this is what happened and I learned a great lesson from this incident.

The moral of this tale is that you never know where your next customer may come from. What this means is that you must always be 'looking your best'. You must always have a friendly face. Moodiness is absolutely forbidden. Patience and tolerance and watchfulness over your behaviour, whether in your place of business or at home, are paramount.

The dear little old lady you help – perhaps supplying her with your product for free because she cannot afford it – could well have a wealthy nephew. When he hears how kind you have been to his aunt, he may decide to buy from you on the strength of your reported kindness, when matched against his present supplier, who happens to have just been rude to him.

So while this idea isn't really an item of specific advice, it represents a principle that you must be on your toes and behave well to everyone (customers, suppliers, tax officials and insurance salespeople, even burglar alarm salespeople) because you never know where your next customer is going to come from. As the business guru, Robert Townsend, says, 'Marketing is *everything* you do.'

32 Have a mission statement

In the past we used to groan when it was suggested that every business should have a mission statement, but, as time has passed, this concept has become more widely accepted. Yes, I accept that it sounds like an American idea, but don't let's moan about and knock every idea that may come from the other side of the pond – and don't let's knock this one.

First of all, what is it? Well, mission statements are short, memorable and believable sentences that encapsulate what it is that your business stands for. I actually think they should be drafted in a way that the customers, as well as the employees, can read and, if they find they are true, accept.

Why have them? Because they summarise why you go to work. So often, people go to work simply to earn a crust. What I would like to see is people going to work to *live*; going to work to enjoy themselves, have fun and spread a little happiness each day both within their organisation and, more importantly, in the direction of their customers. Having a mission statement (at least having the right mission statement) can facilitate such an atmosphere.

You will probably be fed up with me harping on about my own experiences but it's these experiences that have given me the confidence to write this book – they are, I believe, important enough to share with you. In our business, we use the mission statement 'We want to score ten out of ten in everything we do for our clients.' We don't always achieve this score but, when we do, we get thank yous ('wows') accordingly.

This mission statement, which reflects our mission in our working life, is at the head of everyone's employment contract – if people don't believe it, they don't sign up to it and don't come to work for us. It's also measurable. We can ask our customers to rate us against this target, so we can tell how well or badly we're doing. It becomes a core belief and our reason for coming to work.

I happen to think that it's a particularly good one (not that I invented it, but the moment someone said it, I knew it was a winner) and you are welcome to use/plagiarise it.

But perhaps you can see that having a slogan like this provides a happy focus for everything you do at work, is easily remembered and, to counteract the criticisms of the moaners I mentioned at the start of this point, having a mission statement is actually rather a good idea.

33 Work out what it is that you really sell

This is one of those points I have included in this book that I would love to complete by telling you what I think you should do, but, as you will see, only you will be able to work this one out.

The classic explanation of what I'm saying is the one regarding electric drills. When we go into a hardware store and buy a drill, the drill is *not* what we really want. We want the hole that we're going to make with the drill. The drill itself is the means to an end, but the 'why' of why we're buying it is the end product.

Now, to arrive at what you are really selling, you have to think outside the box. You have to defocus your thoughts and contemplate what your product provides for your customers.

It could be something almost negative. As an accountant, just about the only time we know we have a problem on our hands is when a customer is worried (when the taxman is getting at him, or his Tax Return is late, or we have taken too long in preparing his accounts). So we have to ensure that these problems never crop up or if they do, we take the sting out of the situation. As my business partner, Tim Smith, says, 'We are in the business of selling peace of mind' and if we fail to deliver *this* to our customers, we would be failing in our job.

Can you see beyond your brochure and work out what your customers really want? If you can, then not only should all your marketing be directed at this target, but also you may be able to put the price up. If you are selling something that is very similar to your competitors' products but you pitch your marketing in such a way that your product actually appears to do the job better (it does or guarantees something that your rivals' don't appear to sell or provide), you will find that customers prefer your goods and will be prepared to pay more for them.

As I say, it's impossible for me to refer to your particular sector, especially when I don't know you, but why not ask your customers or employees, or even your competitors, and search for something that will really hit the button – and tell the world the unique thing that you sell.

Word will soon spread.

34 Ask your employees what they think

This is so important – yet it took me years to spot.

Your employees probably have a better view of your business than you do. This may surprise you but it's true. It's true because they are not you. I assume it was you who started this business or if you didn't, you are now running it and so the business, whether you like it or not, is an extension of your personality. Its philosophies will be yours and while we may not understand this fully, we can never stand outside our own self or the way we practise our philosophies. Others, and especially employees, have a much better understanding of this because they can actually see you in action. They can observe you and your business better than you can.

Customers obviously have the best vantage point when it comes to assessing a business and indeed they have the only viewpoint that matters because, on their assessment of what they see, they will decide whether or not to buy. However, employees have a view that is nearly as good as the customers'.

I decided to ask my employees for their opinions on the business as a whole and on its future direction, and suggested that we should spend an afternoon at a neutral venue to discuss an agenda that they would help create.

How did they play a part in creating the agenda? Well, I circulated a nine-point questionnaire for them to complete before we assembled. Here are some of the questions I asked:

1. What's the best part of your job?

2. What's the worst part of your job?

3. How long would you like to work in this business?

4. What ambitions do you have in this firm?

5. What work do you like doing?

6. What do you not like doing?

7. What would you like to be doing?

8. What changes do you think we should make to the way the business is run?

9. What further training would you like?

I collected the answers together and amalgamated them onto one sheet of paper, then we went though the answers at a meeting with our employees one by one.

It made a profound difference to the whole direction of the business. In fact, it resulted in us moving premises, which was a good idea, but it also made staff realise that their contribution was valued and respected. It also made me realise just how much those who worked in the business cared about the business and wanted to see it prosper.

35 Avoid small print

(I have a feeling that the title of this point is a euphemism for 'avoid lawyers'!)

This is such an obvious point and yet so many businesses spend lots of time and money creating the small print that they believe will protect them, but this creates deep mistrust on the part of the customer.

To create an air of credibility when making a deal with a customer, do emphasise that you want to be fair to both parties. Once the customer has paid you, stress how well you will be looking after him and the benefits he will be receiving. This is how to get customers to love you. The more these benefits gets piled on top of your clients, the sooner they will forget what they have paid you and will consider your prices to be a great deal.

However, if you start by threatening your customers with interest and legal action in your small print, why should they ever buy anything from you?

So if you have a customer service agreement with pages of legalese and impenetrable small print, tear it all up and start again.

36 An example of how to avoid unfriendly small print

The following example shows you how my accountancy firm treats our clients when it comes to their annual Tax Return service. All the small print is beneficial to the customer and not to their detriment.

INVOICE No: 2013/0125	
Fee for our services in connection with your 2013 Tax Return:	£165.00
VAT @ 20%:	£33.00
Total due by 31 May 2013:	£198.00

The way our annual Tax Return service works is as follows: if you would kindly settle this invoice by 31 May 2013 and send us your

Tax Return papers by 30 June 2013, in return we will:

- complete your 2013 Tax Return and send it to you for review, signing and for it to be returned to us;

- tell you how much tax you will have to pay when we send you your Tax Return;

- file your Tax Return electronically and let you know as soon as we receive acknowledgement from HM Revenue & Customs that it has been processed (so you need not even begin to worry about automatic penalties);

- send you a payslip for submitting with your tax cheque, should you require one;

- chase you if you don't get on with it (the chasing will begin on 1 July);

- send you copies of all our newsletters during the year (including the fastest Budget newsletter there is!);

- for a one-off payment, look after all of this for you for a period of 12 months up to 30 April 2014.

In addition:

If HM Revenue & Customs enquire into your Tax Return, so long as you have sent us your papers on time, we guarantee that you will not pay a penny for our fees in this connection. In our experience, enquiries normally average £1,000 in accountancy fees but, for you, there will be no charge.

You can correspond with us by Freepost and pay by credit card or Standing Order.

You can enjoy the free use of one of our Taxafiles (your own personal Tax Return organiser).

You can telephone, write, email or fax us at any stage about your Tax Return and there are no extra charges. This is an all-inclusive fee.

Because the Tax Return work is handled by team members whom we both train and value, in many cases the letter accompanying the Tax Return will be signed by the person who carried out the work.

In other words, we are all at your service.

This price does not include accounts preparation, other professional work not directly connected to the Tax Return nor work by an outside specialist adviser (should this be required). We also reserve the right to charge extra for any major Capital Gains Tax work, should this also be required, but we would only do so if you agreed that an extra charge was appropriate.

We don't believe that we have put off our customers with our small print.

37 Make sure that your signs don't put off your customers

One of the most irritating signs one can see when driving into a professional firm's car park is 'parking space reserved for senior partner'. Equally off-putting is 'keep off the grass' and that simply awful one, 'cars and contents left entirely at owner's risk'.

Why are the people who put these signs there so insensitive? They hate these signs when they see them on other people's premises, yet they put them up on their own and it's a real no-no.

When I was looking for new office premises and was with the landlord visiting the suite that we eventually decided to rent, he said to me, 'There are three parking spaces right outside your front door.' My immediate response was 'Good. They will be for our clients.' He said my reaction reflected his own customer service philosophy and we became firm friends from that moment.

In fact, later he put up a sign reserving the parking spaces for our firm. This created a bit of a problem for me – he had put the signs up to stop people parking there from other firms, but the signs read as if the parking spaces were reserved for the partners. So we altered the signs to say that they were for *visitors* to our firm.

You do need signs – to tell first-time visitors where you work – but these signs must be customer-friendly and not something your lawyer has invented to save your backside if there's a problem.

There are two golf courses near Brecon in Wales that are within three miles of each other. At one, as you arrive, you will see over ten signs that fall within this category and they all start with 'don't'. They are a real turn-off. At the other, the first sign you see is 'welcome'.

Which golf course would you rather visit?

38 Create an organisation chart

Filling in one of these will tell you if you have a business. If you have a number of different names for those who fulfil the different roles, you know you have a business. If your name fills every box, then you should start employing others to help you create a business because at present you simply have a job. Please refer to the chart on the following pages.

39 Have a vision statement

A vision statement is a short (no more than one page) statement of what you want your business to look like in (say) five years' time.

Here is a typical template for you to develop in your own way. I've added some suggested words to fill the blanks:

Working Vision Statement

This firm has as its sole commercial purpose the objective of _____.

It will be acknowledged as the _____best_____ in its industry and region.

Team members will be _____proud_____ to be part of the firm and will benefit from _____above_____ average compensation, a _____happy_____ working environment, _____constant_____ opportunity for professional advancement and personal growth and _____a close_____ involvement in the decision-making process within the firm.

There will be a _____high_____ level of trust and mutual respect amongst all team members, owners and clients.

Organisation Chart for _____

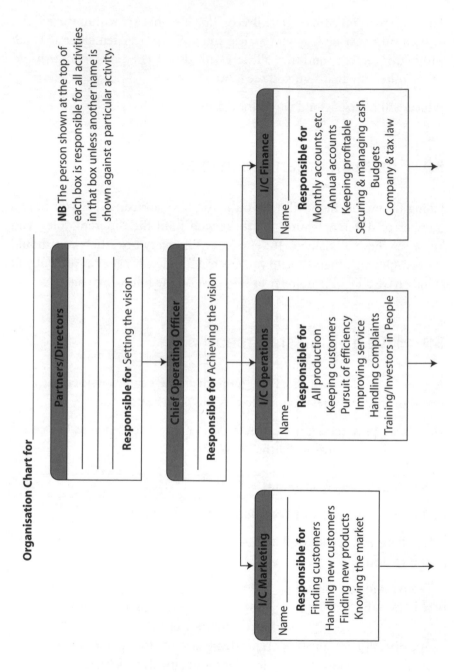

NB The person shown at the top of each box is responsible for all activities in that box unless another name is shown against a particular activity.

Partners/Directors

_____
_____
_____

Responsible for Setting the vision

Chief Operating Officer

_____

Responsible for Achieving the vision

I/C Marketing

Name _____

Responsible for
Finding customers
Handling new customers
Finding new products
Knowing the market

I/C Operations

Name _____

Responsible for
All production
Keeping customers
Pursuit of efficiency
Improving service
Handling complaints
Training/Investors in People

I/C Finance

Name _____

Responsible for
Monthly accounts, etc.
Annual accounts
Keeping profitable
Securing & managing cash
Budgets
Company & tax law

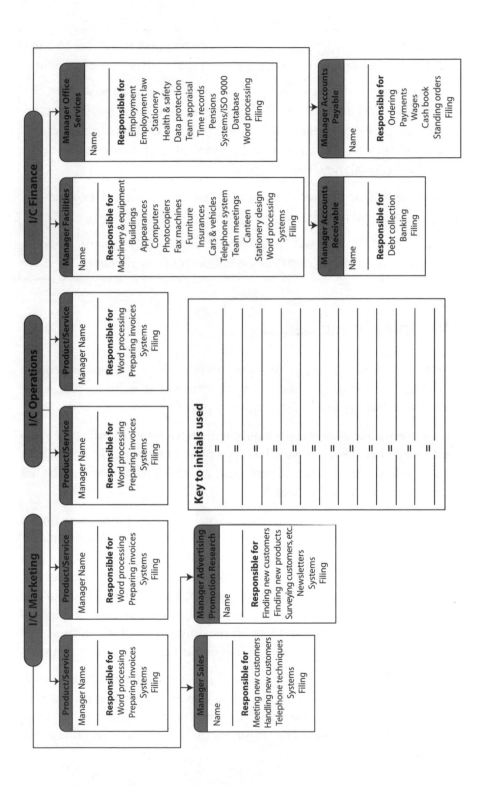

Each person _____will_____ understand and subscribe to the firm's mission and will ___regularly___ assist in its accomplishment.

The owners of the firm will _____always_____ place the welfare of the firm and that of its clients above their own self-interests. However, it will always be understood that the owners can expect to receive fair compensation reflecting the value of their contribution and the capital they have invested.

The firm will be innovative in its service delivery and will be guided by its principal purpose of ___always wanting to excel___.

The service it offers will be clearly defined, highly structured and priced in accordance to the value it represents to its clients.

40 Think 'value added'

We all tend to think that price is the driving force behind most people's purchases and that we have to be the cheapest if we're to please our customers, but as I said previously, this is a fallacy.

Yes, agreed, none of us like paying more than we want to, but, at the same time, we all like the extras we get when we buy something. How often have we, or indeed our friends, said how great it is that a particular product has come with an extra component?

When I bought a car from a particular manufacturer for the first time, I was amazed at all the extras that came with it. Indeed, it took my son, then aged 11, and me, a new customer, three months to discover all the hidden extras that the manufacturer had developed (things such as seat heaters, cup holders, a pocket stitched to the front of the driver's seat to put bits and pieces in, etc.). My car is a good example of how these thoughtful additions are the things that make all the difference and it's on these that we should be concentrating when we plan our customer service strategy.

If we stick with the car analogy, most if not all cars get you from A to B, but if you buy a car and find that it also cossets you while it performs its main function, doesn't that draw you towards it compared to the other makes you know less well? The reason for this attraction is the value added extras.

I don't know about cars, but from observation I have seen that, on the whole, these value added extras are not expensive for the manufacturer (service provider, etc.) to supply. But it's these facets that make a product stand out from the competition and make it more valuable to the customer.

This, after all, is what value added is all about. It's seen as a valuable additional feature to the customer (an extra something that he considers highly desirable; something that adds value in his eyes), but, in the context of the whole production exercise, it has cost you (in relative terms) peanuts to provide.

Could you supply more value added features to your product or service?

41 Cutting costs is not necessarily the best way

I start this point with a slightly heavy heart because there is an inevitability about the need to be always looking at costs and cutting them where they are not necessary. If you run a business where everything is pared to the bone, it can create an air of possible alarm, but certainly despondency because all the participants feel that they are on too tight a leash.

My belief is that business grows more by being nice to your customers than by buying the cheapest there is. Indeed, the whole ethos of this book is that we should all be striving to be the best and the best isn't cheap. So if you buy cheap materials and resources, it's unlikely that your end product will be top price (your product will reflect the cheapness of the goods that have gone into it to make it) and your profits will tend to be lower as a result.

I won't bang on about this point because, as I say, there is a logic to saving money wherever one can, but my preference is to try to increase sales than cut costs.

42 Try an advert

After saying that I'm not a huge fan of adverts (although if I were to spend money on an advert it would be in the *Yellow Pages*), advertising is a fact of life and most of us do it.

The essence of this point is that while some of your work colleagues will be negative about a proposed advertisement, you don't know if they are right until you try it out.

There is no law that says one certain sort of advert works and another doesn't. It's a bit of a toss up. Indeed, it's arrogant to say that something won't work, unless you have tried it.

43 The four phases of owning an elephant

This point is less about growing your business and more about illustrating what tends to go wrong in business and what to do about it.

Phase 1

You buy a baby elephant. You are bigger than it is, can see a great future with it and foresee no problems. The only problem is that you don't have any skills in managing elephants – but you think that this won't matter and off you go.

Phase 2

The elephant soon grows much bigger than you. You are no longer strong enough to control it and it takes over your whole life. It pulls you along, wreaking destruction in its wake. Standing behind it, it blocks your whole vision and you can neither see nor know where you are going. You are so preoccupied by being dragged along by it that you think there is no way to ever bring it under control. it's ruining your and your family's quality of life. (Most people get stuck right here. Does this sound familiar?)

Phase 3

You are one of the rare ones who decides to take advice on how to become a pukka elephant handler or mahout. You realise that in order to control your elephant, it's no use walking behind it ineffectually holding onto the reins as it pulls you along. You accept that you have to take a wholly different approach and that you have to learn how to manage your elephant to get the most out of it. To do this, you have to know how to sit on top of your elephant, where you can not only see where you are going, but also, with just a gentle touch with your feet on its ears, steer the elephant in the direction you want it to go. In a short time you are now running the elephant instead of it running (and ruining) your life. As a result of accepting that you need help, and as a result of taking professional advice, it is soon fulfilling your original dreams.

Phase 4

Once you have learned how to control your elephant, and it won't take long, you can then hire and train your own mahout to manage the elephant for you, while you ride in the canopied howdah behind, sitting back and enjoying the view. In addition, you can sell your fully trained elephant for a handsome profit.

44 Work with your neighbours

There are two reasons why it's a good idea to work closely with your business neighbours:

1. They may become customers.

2. They may introduce customers to you.

So:

- invite them in for a coffee;

- invite them to office parties;

- tell them what you are doing – put them on your mailing list for newsletters, etc.;

- ask them what they are doing – you might be able to introduce business to them and that might encourage reciprocal introductions;

- ask them if they want a lift in your car to work;

- ask them if they'd like to see around your premises;

- ask them if they would like to share their database with you and vice versa;

- you might even be able to do some joint marketing, even though you may have very different businesses.

In other words, neighbours could well be a very valuable source of new business if you treat them well.

45 A tribute to my business hero Robert Townsend

It was in 1970 that I read Robert Townsend's book, *Up the Organisation*, and I'm sorry that I lent my first edition to someone and never got it back.

The book was a revelation and an exciting read. Was this how a business should be run? It made such sense and yet it was so alien to what I had ever experienced at work or read before. I have tried to follow his maxims ever since and I hope this book is a reliable reflection of his inspiring philosophy.

What did Robert Townsend say? There isn't enough space here to explain (and, in any event, I suggest you try to get hold of a copy – I see amazon.co.uk have a few copies available) but here are a few gems from a taped interview he recorded:

- The best way to do business is to have fun doing it.

- Concentrate on a few goals. Most businesses try to do too much.

- The job of the leader is to liberate his team so that 80 per cent of their time is spent working towards their chosen goals.

- Cut out unnecessary meetings and unnecessary memos.

- Have the guts to do things differently.

- Job descriptions, if they have to be written down, should be written by the employee.

- Empower as much as possible everyone who works for you.

- A new manager, on arrival, should ask everyone for ideas on improving the business.

- Employing new people should always be on the basis of a 90-day trial period.

- Mistakes are an essential part of success.

- When assessing new ventures use the 'yes, yes principle'. If you can say yes to these two questions, then you must try it:

  - Is what we are trying to do in line with our business goals?

  - If it fails in the worst possible way, can we afford it?

- Don't keep people in the same job for too long.

- If the meeting really ought to be short, hold it standing up.

- People in understaffed businesses feel less of a sense of job insecurity and so are more relaxed.

- If someone has to be dismissed, remember that you are not trying to punish him. You are just trying to get the organisation straight. It's always better to be generous to the person leaving, don't damage their self-esteem and help them find a new posting.

- Don't have personal secretaries – secretaries should all be in a typing pool.

And, as I've already quoted:

- Marketing is everything you do.

46 How to set about changing things in your business – an agenda for a mini planning session

In this sample agenda, I'm going to deal with the 18 Great Leverage Points. (These were taught to me by my good friend Paul Dunn, who used to run Results Accountants Network.)

In my experience, using this agenda has never failed to produce a successful meeting.

Mini Planning Session

Agenda for meeting at _____

1. **There are just four ways to grow a business**

    We can:

    a. increase the number of customers of the sort we want;

    b. increase the number of times they do business with us;

    c. increase the average value;

    d. increase our own effectiveness at doing the work that we do.

    What can we do to achieve improvements in this area?

2. **What you can measure you can manage**

    Here we need ideas for identifying whether our business is growing. The first is obviously the number of customers, but can anybody think of any other ways in which we can measure whether the business is going forward? See point 80.

3. **The true purpose of any advertisement is to get a response**

    a. How effective is our advertising?

    b. Is there any other advertising we could do?

4. **Build in unique core differentiators, focus on them and articulate them constantly**

    What is it that our business does really well? In particular, is there something that other, similar businesses don't do (because that is the bit we want to get across)?

5. **Look for a second dimension**

    Do we know any other businesses that we could link up with?

6. **Learn to really listen**

    Are we asking our customers enough?

Let's organise a customer survey or advisory board to ask our customers the following:

- What they think of us.

- What we are doing right.

- What we are doing wrong.

- What we ought to be doing.

7. **Cutting the price is always an easy option but there is usually a better way**

   We should think of increasing the value that we give rather than reducing the price.

8. **Lowering the barriers to doing business**

   Here we need to consider what it is that might prevent non-customers from crossing our threshold. Is parking a barrier?

9. **The more you tell the more you sell**

   Are we telling our customers enough about our business?

10. **Avoid changing horses in midstream**

    The idea here is that after the meeting we should start a plan that we stick to for at least three months, preferably much longer. In other words, it's important for everybody sitting around the table to own the idea so that we really run with it confidently for a long enough period to see if it does work.

11. **What's in it for me? (WIIFM)**

    We know that our business is extremely good at caring for its customers. Therefore, in any advertisement, menu, newsletter, etc. we must identify the WIIFM factor and work on it.

    [*Your mentor, as an outsider and potential customer, may be able to offer ideas here.*]

12. Learn the key frustrations

Most businesses are guilty of driving their customers mad. In the case of our business, it might be not serving the customers quickly enough. Only a customer advisory board will really find out what the frustrations are, but I'm sure we can offer ideas under this heading. The idea is that we identify what all the other businesses in our industry get wrong and then eliminate them.

13. Systematise

A really effective business is one that operates in a systematic way. Preferably, there should be written procedures so that every time we look after a client, he gets the same treatment.

How standardised are our procedures? Is there a way in which they could be systematised better?

14. Empowering our team

This is a very important subject and means recognising the ability that exists amongst our team members, giving them full responsibility and watching them develop, grow and enjoy working for us even more.

15. Don't reverse the risk; remove it

What are the risks that our customers run when they do business with us and can we address them?

What sort of guarantees can we give?

16. Give people a clear and detailed action plan

This will develop from the need for the proprietors to have developed a long-term goal. This goal needs to be declared and owned by everybody. Once that happens, we build a long-term action plan, using Key Performance Indicators to see how well we are going along the path, then everybody can use this as a map to see how successful the business is.

17. **Create offers to add value and to encourage quicker responses**

    Are there any offers that we could make?

18. **Adding the third dimension**

    The basic question here is, 'Which other companies have the customers that we are trying to reach?'

    The crux of the matter is that our potential clients are already customers of other businesses. If we can think of firms that have those customers, could we develop joint ventures with those companies to gain access to those clients?

47 Eight things to do to improve profitability

There are many ways in which the essence of this book could be summed up. I believe that point 100 is the best set of instructions but these following points can also be followed:

1. Start by holding a meeting as suggested in the last point.

2. Identify the opportunities to be exploited.

3. Set up an agenda for the work to be done, i.e. an action plan.

4. Work with your customers to find out what they want you to do.

5. Work with your team to discover their ideas.

6. Redesign your organisational structure if necessary (see page 40).

7. Set up Key Performance Indicators (see point 80) so that you can measure what's going on and watch things improve.

8. Monitor these every month.

48 What an action plan looks like

There are two types of action plan, but they both aim at a target – action followed by results.

The first, and more important, plan concerns those things that you are going to start doing now (the list of top priorities – are you creating one on page xiv?) The second is the list of those things that you will do one day, which I hope that you are compiling on page xv. (They may not be urgent but you don't want to lose sight of them.) So the top priorities have to be attended to first.

Now, please feel free to tweak this – for it to work you have to be happy with the plan itself, but, in principle, I believe the first action plan should look like this:

List of Top Priorities		
Action (Description)	By Whom (Who Is Responsible for Achieving These Points)	By When

The list of **Second Priorities** would be similar:		
Action (Description)	Initial Responsibility Lies with	Possible Date for Completion

And then, once you have achieved an action, it's very important to have a list of points that have been dealt with. This way everyone can see that this whole process is really achieving things of value. It will add momentum to the process.

List of Actions Completed

Action (Description)	Date Completed	By Whom

49 A simple business plan template

It would be strange in a book of this nature not to mention what a business plan might look like. Please note that a business plan isn't an action plan. A business plan might be needed if you are seeking an outside investor, bank finance or perhaps applying for Investors in People status (a framework for a business's improvement through its people).

Here is a list of suggested contents for such a business plan:

Business Profile

Business Overview & Mission Statement	Provide a general outline of your business, so that outsiders will understand what your business is all about.
Unique Features	Discuss the advantage that gives you the edge in the market. What are you doing that others aren't?
Sales Overview	Show in tabular form your recent sales figures.
Sales Forecast	Show projected sales and profits for the next three years.
Proof of Sales	Show some evidence that your projections will come to fruition.

Competitive Profile

Market Size	What is the total market and is it growing?

Market Segments	Try to break the market down into smaller segments and show how your product fits into that segment.
Market Trends	Show what is happening to your market that will affect your business.
Competitive Analysis	How do you compare with your competitors?

Strategic Direction

SWOT Analysis	Write down in four tables your strengths, weaknesses, opportunities and threats.
Vision Statement	This is a concise statement of where you want to be in three, five and ten years' time.
Target Market	Give examples of to whom exactly you will be selling your products and services.
Positioning	How will you position your products? Is there a gap in the market? What benefits will you be selling?
Strategy Highlights	What are the major things you will need in order to achieve your financial targets?
Investor Information	What do you want to borrow and what return on their investment can your investors expect?

The Actual Plan

Business Objectives	You simply state, 'We want to sell £X,000 per year at a gross profit of Y per cent, resulting in a net profit of Z per cent.'
Marketing Plan	In detail, with costs and timescale, how are you going to market your product?
Financial Plan	In summary, how and when is the money going to come in and out? Use a simple spreadsheet including the details in the next section.

| Organisational Plan | In detail, who is going to do what and when? |
| Any Other Plans | Include any other relevant plans you have (including your current action plan). |

Financials

First-Year Budget	This is where your accountant can really help.
First-Year Cash-Flow	See above.
Five-Year Budget	See above.
Five-Year Sales Forecast	See above.
Five-Year Balance Sheets	See above.

Implementation

This section is only completed when the business has something to report. It can be ignored if the business has yet to start.

| Milestones | A list of who is going to do what and when and, importantly, a record of whether this has been done. |
| Actual | A comparison of budgets with actual performance. |

Essentials for your customers

50 Proper coffee

This is one of the cheapest and one of the best ways to win customers. In fact, it doesn't have to be coffee, but the concept of proper coffee makes the point.

Most people (including me) like the aroma of roasting coffee beans, so why not benefit from this 'turn on' and provide a really good cup of proper coffee with cups and saucers (as well as matching sugar bowl and milk jug) when visitors call.

Also, offer your customers a wide range of teas (e.g. Earl Grey and Lapsang Souchong) as well as a choice of juices, which will be particularly popular in hot weather. Why not offer really good biscuits (buns even) and just see how visitors react!

If you are in any doubt as to what to provide, ask your customers what they would like to eat and drink and let them lead the way. You could even take it one step further and make a note of what customers ask for when they visit and keep it in their files, so when they call again, you can offer them the same.

You will soon get a name for the civilised way you treat visitors to your premises. This very civility which you exude will, of itself, lead to higher prices as your customers will be happy with price increases if they are getting a good service. But if you stick to chipped and tired mugs, or even those dreadful plastic cups, why on earth should your clients pay you a premium price when you treat them so shoddily? I think proper coffee should be high on everyone's customer service strategy.

51 Service is far more important than product

This is one of Pizza Express' maxims. I probably don't need to say anything more but it wouldn't be a bad thing to add a word of embellishment.

So often we focus on the product but forget that, while we're beavering away, there is a customer who is fed up with waiting for us to finish the job. So we give him his repaired shoes, and, yes, they have been wonderfully repaired but he'll never darken our doors again because we took too long to do the job.

52 What does great service cost?

I hope that I may be forgiven for talking about cars again, but I had a grim car experience when I suffered a puncture outside Maidenhead. The wheel with the flat tyre was jammed on. For the life of me I couldn't loosen it. So I phoned a number of garages in Maidenhead for help but all of them replied, 'No, sorry mate. It's late in the day and we're all going home'.

Well, the tyre was ruined anyway so I limped into the town and found a back street garage that was prepared to down tools and help me change my tyre.

The next day, I went to Central Tyre on the A30 at Egham to get the tyre problem sorted, and as I drove in I saw the words 'unbeaten on service' on their rotating sign. I like to think that I know a little about service so I wondered how good they really were.

Later that day, when I returned to collect the new tyre and after I had talked with a number of people at the garage, I said to the man giving me the bill, 'As I arrived this morning I saw your sign about providing great service and I wondered whether you meant it. I have to say that you have done brilliantly and I want to compliment and thank you all for the great way I have been looked after'. I will never forget what the man said in reply, 'Wow. Thank you, sir. And, do you know, that bit doesn't cost us anything?'

There you have it. Great service costs either nothing or next to nothing but the rewards that flow from it are immense. It's the epitome of that Biblical saying, 'It's better to give than to receive'. When you give you get far more back than you ever parted with.

53 Don't charge by the hour (customers really hate it)

It always amazes me that we, in the Western world, still charge our customers by the hour. Now, in case you are surprised or worried by this initial comment, please just ask yourself, 'Do I like being charged by the hour?' I'd be very surprised if you do. When we hear that the job will be charged by the hour, we usually tend to ask, 'How many hours will it take and what is your hourly charge?' and, if we're given those two imponderables, we then need to do some maths and see if we can afford the bill. If we're not told the amount of time it will take and the rate per hour, then we simply haven't got a clue what the final bill will be – anymore, perhaps, than the person selling you his services. (In fact, he isn't just selling you his services; he is also selling you his time and so, in a way, you are becoming his employer, not his customer.)

The point about charging by the hour is that the risk is taken entirely by the customer; if you are charged in this way, can you be sure that the right number of hours and minutes have been written down? (If you ask me, very few people record their time honestly and any bill based on hours taken is, almost invariably, wrong.) The whole business of charging by the hour is incredibly customer-unfriendly and if I were Prime Minister, I'd outlaw it. Think how it would make the lawyers scream and squirm!

When you work in an industry that tends to charge by the hour, please try to set up a system of quoting upfront for your work. If you do, you will find that you can charge more. Let's say that you are facing a customer and he is asking you what the charge will be (better still, you have already said to that customer, 'Would you like me to quote for this service?'). You reckon up roughly how long the job will take, multiply the sum by your hourly rate, add in something for unforeseen delays, etc. and say, 'We will charge £X for this service. We normally charge for our services upfront, but, having billed upfront, we're happy to be paid by Standing Order. If the charge is acceptable, we would like to tell you of our three guarantees:

1.   If you are not satisfied with our service, you are entitled to ask for up to a full refund and you are the only judge.

2.   We guarantee to finish this work within eight weeks, but if you

would like it to be completed sooner, let me know and we'll try our best to meet your preferred deadline.

3. Miss X will be in charge of this matter, she works every day except Monday and her extension number is XXXX.

This approach removes all the risk and will amaze and delight your customers.

However you do it, please don't charge by the hour and remember this little ditty:

When accountants and solicitors charge by the hour
Clients moan about fees and relationships sour
So throw away time sheets – fix price all you do
Bill 'em upfront and clients will love you!

Believe me, it's true. Just do it!

54 If no-one else is doing it, that's a sure sign you should seriously consider setting them an example

What I'm getting at here is that humans tend to behave like sheep. We all flock together and few step outside and do things differently.

I know that I, myself, am guilty of this crime. For years I knew that there was something wrong with billing by the hour. Our clients obviously hated it, it brought untold problems for us, it took time (recording all those hours and processing the time sheets) but everyone else in our profession did it and so we kept going with it too.

In our bones we knew it was a mad system but we did nothing about it. We behaved like sheep and, as the boss of my firm, I was the chief sheep. But once we stepped outside of the apparent comfort zone of time recording, things really started to happen. We won great new contracts, we won awards and we enjoyed real exhilaration in our work.

How long did we wait before this happened? Well, we started the business in 1973 and we didn't finally drop time recording until 2000. So it took us 27 years to step outside our comfort zone.

What might have happened if we'd done this ten years earlier? Who knows? I'm ashamed that it took me so long to pluck up courage to make this change from what the rest of my profession were doing – and in many cases still are.

What's niggling you about the way you currently do business? Try that new method you've had bugging you for all these years. Step outside your comfort zone and watch life take off.

55 Give introducer rewards

This can be tricky. Some professions prohibit their members paying any sort of reward or commission to introducers so you may need to tread carefully.

However, in principle, there appears to be nothing wrong with offering your existing customers a certain defined reward for introductions. For example, if you are a chiropractor, you could say to all existing customers in your monthly mailing, 'Next month we are having a special promotion. If you book yourself in for a consultation and bring a friend with you who isn't already a patient of ours, we will treat you both for half price.'

In our business, where we have written a number of consumer awareness guides, we can offer both the existing client and the person he is introducing a free copy each of one of our guides. It may not be that exciting, but you can bet it's more than other firms in our area are doing!

Wine merchants often offer a free bottle of wine for each successful introduction. Could you take a leaf out of their book? They wouldn't be offering this sort of incentive if it didn't work.

Obviously, you want the reward to be:

- commensurate – in line with the kindness they are doing for you;

- valuable – worth it for them; for the time and trouble they are taking; and

- not tacky – offering £25 to existing customers for successful introductions may come over as demeaning. They may be so wealthy that £25 is beneath them.

So this needs careful thought. Nonetheless, it may be worth thinking about how you might reward those who bring you business. After all, such introductions have cost you very little.

But whatever you do, at the very least you must always remember to say thank you to those who introduce new clients. Indeed, you must have a system for doing this. If someone introduces work to you and you fail to thank him, he might easily say, 'Well, that's the last time I'll do that for them.'

If you think about it, you usually find that advertising is costly and often totally ineffective. Yet we continue to spend huge sums each year on it. Would it not make better sense to spend less on advertising and more on rewarding those who introduce customers to us?

56 Turn up on time

This is one idea that others are beginning to cotton on to. I have already talked about washing machine repair people not coming when they said they would. Indeed, we may already know of people who have taken a day off work to be at home when someone calls to do something important and then never turns up. Such behaviour is outrageous.

Now, if you can guarantee to turn up on time and you mention this in your advertisements, you will be offering something that very few businesses offer and you will get more enquiries. It's very important to describe your guarantees in your advertisements because if you don't acknowledge their existence, it could undermine your selling points. Let me explain:

If you have a problem with a supplier and you refuse to pay him, and he takes you to court and you win, he won't get paid for the work that you were dissatisfied with. So this trader, with no overt guarantees, has provided you with a built-in guarantee, albeit unwillingly, whereby you have not had to pay for work with which you were unsatisfied. In this respect, the law provides all customers with a guarantee, if they want to use it.

But if you say upfront that 'if we mess you about, leave your kitchen filthy, don't turn up on time, don't do the job properly, we will put things right at our expense', you are stating openly, clearly and honestly that the customer has an ultimate guarantee of satisfaction. This makes you look so much more customer-friendly than someone who offers no guarantees and whom you have to fight if you want reparation.

57 Do unheard of things

This is a difficult point to write because, if the things I'm suggesting you do have never been heard of before, how have I heard of them? The short answer is that I haven't – so any action you take as a result of reading this point is going to be down to you. However, let me tell you of something unheard of that we did in our accountancy practice (in fact, it's a number of things):

As I have said at point 53, clients who use professional advisers hate being charged by the hour, so my business has stopped doing this, but we have discovered other unheard of things as well. I think the best way to explain this is to go straight to the finishing line.

A few years ago, we won a national award for customer service. We went up to a posh hotel and when the announcer told the hundreds in the banqueting hall that we had won the award, he said that the following elements of our submission were unique. These were that we:

- billed upfront;
- never charged by the hour; and
- (as mentioned before) offered a no-quibble guarantee that said (and still says), 'If you are not satisfied with our service, it's quite simple, you don't pay and you are the only judge.'

We think that's how everyone in business should behave but in 2001 it was described as being 'unheard of'. Now, you are most welcome to crib this guarantee of ours – it's yours for the taking – but does this tale encourage you to think of offering something 'unheard of' to your customers?

If this leaves you thoughtless, just ask the next customer you meet, 'What can we do for you that would make all the difference?' and then, when he makes a request, try to match, or even better, it.

Sorry not to be more helpful over this point, but this one has to be down to you!

58 Increase the number of customers

Now, some of you may be getting itchy feet because just about everything I've covered so far has involved the soft approach. Yes, it's all good sense and laudable, but it hasn't really cut to the numbers. While this point doesn't get very far into the numbers themselves, it should please those who want to see how the figures work out.

I'm going to take an imaginary business with 100 regular customers who spend £100 per year, making the annual turnover £10,000. I'm going to assume that the costs of sale (those directly related to the product, such as materials, delivery, etc.) are £6,000 and the overheads a further £3,000; the business therefore makes a net profit of £1,000 or ten per cent of its turnover.

These figures may not relate to your business, but the proportions are not untypical and you should be able to use the table below as a template.

What I'm going to do is see what happens if you could, as this point says, 'increase the number of customers'. I'm going to play with a ten per cent increase – which isn't an unreasonable increase to aim for if you start following some of the ideas included in this book. I'm going to assume that you don't need to incur any extra overheads if you are going to serve ten per cent more customers, but you will incur a proportionate increase in your costs of sales.

Have a look at what happens:

	Existing scenario		Projection after 10% increase	
Number of customers	100		110	
Number of times	1		1	
Average sale	**£100**		**£100**	
Value of sales		10,000		11,000
Costs of sales		**6,000**		**6,600**
Gross profit		4,000		4,400
Overheads		3,000		3,000
Net profit		**£1,000**		**£1,400**

Have you noticed that after an increase of ten per cent in the customer base, the net profit has shot up by 40 per cent? Does this interest you?

The purpose of this first 'go at the maths' is to show you how important it is always to look at new ways of attracting more customers. You may have thought that an increase of ten per cent would only add ten per cent to your profits and it may not be worth while pursuing but, in this case, it's added 40 per cent to the net profit. Bearing in mind that most businesses are valued on the basis of their net profit, it has also added 40 per cent to the value of the business. Not bad, eh? Could this work for you?

59 Increase the number of times your customers do business with you

So we've made a start on working with the figures. Let's see what impact you might be able to make if you could invite your customers to buy from you more than once a year.

It makes sense to use the same scenario as I've used above and I'm going to take up where I left off, having already increased the profits by 40 per cent. What I'm going to do now is imagine what would happen if just five per cent of your customers decide to buy from you one more time a year and, again, I'm assuming that this small increase will not involve you increasing your overheads.

Here is what the figures would indicate:

	After increasing customer numbers		Once 5% of your customers buy from you one more time	
Number of customers	110		110	
Number of times	1		1.05	
Average sale	**£100**		**£100**	
Value of sales		11,000		11,550
Costs of sales		**6,600**		**6,930**
Gross profit		4,400		4,620
Overheads		3,000		3,000
Net profit		**£1,400**		**£1,620**

This shows how you can add a further £220 to your profits, which is a further 22 per cent on your original profit, thereby increasing your profit by 62 per cent.

But how do you get customers to buy from you more often than they currently do? Let me take the example of the small independent garage where I filled up this morning. Now, as you may know, garages make nothing on petrol. This is why they are closing down (small village garages are dying like flies all over the countryside – partly because the credit cards are making more money with each fill up than the poor garage proprietor and partly because the government takes so much in duty). How does this particular man not just survive but prosper? His answer is to have a large shop selling all sorts of things plus a place at the back where do-it-yourself enthusiasts can bring their cars to tinker with them. Were it not for these value added extras, he would have had to close. He makes no money at all on petrol.

So take a leaf out of this man's book; look to see what else you can sell to your customers – and then start doing it.

60 Put the price up (part 2)

I know that I've mentioned doing this before, but I need to put some figures to the test. Again, I'll pick up from where I left off, using the figures we have already seen and with which I hope you feel comfortable. (If you don't use these figures, then create a simple spreadsheet for yourself and put in the percentage changes you would like to use.)

Here, I will put the price up by ten per cent because it makes the figures work nicely and a ten per cent increase is a proportion that most people are happy to implement. Also, because increasing the price is something that doesn't affect overheads, again we don't have to increase them over £3,000.

Have a look and see what effect a ten per cent price increase has:

	From the previous exercise	**After 10% increase**
Number of customers	110	110
Number of times	1	1.05

Average sale	£100		£110	
Value of sales	11,500		12,705	
Costs of sales	6,930		6,930	
Gross profit	4,620		5,775	
Overheads	3,000		3,000	
Net profit	£1,620		£2,775	

The upshot of all this is that, within three pages, I have shown you how to nearly treble your profits in a way that (to my mind) is easily understood – there's no rocket science involved. At the same time, I have also nearly trebled the value of the business I have been working on.

There is, of course, one objection to this: I hear you saying, 'But my customers will never stomach a ten per cent increase; they will all leave.'

Now, some may go elsewhere, but if you look back to the earlier point where we considered putting the price up (point 23), you will notice that if your gross profit is 40 per cent (as it is here), you would have to lose 20 per cent of your customers before you are back to your previous level of profits and I have never known this to happen. Even if you were to lose 20 per cent, you would still be making the same level of profit but for only 80 per cent of the effort. So putting the price up really is a win-win situation.

Could you put these three elements together and achieve a remarkable increase in profits?

61 The benefit of customer 'wows'

This idea may surprise you but I think 'wows' from customers are very important.

I'll start with moans by customers. Let's face it, when they arrive, and whether they are justified or not, they drain morale. We have to deal with them and they can take a disproportionate amount of time and energy. They can bring anyone's working day to a halt.

If they make us angry and we vent our spleen on the customers concerned (which isn't the way to deal with customer complaints), these moans can seriously damage our business and its reputation.

This point is meant to be an antidote to such problems and a wake-up call to value and use customer 'wows' properly.

A 'wow' is when a customer says not just 'thank you' but 'you were wonderful'. He can do this in a number of ways: by sending you a letter, calling you up or simply by saying thank you effusively as he walks away from your premises.

Just as we're urged to write down, log and deal with customer complaints systematically, I believe that we should record customer 'wows' and milk them for all we can. For example, just as moans have to be shared around your place of work, you should share 'wows' as well. If your employees care about their place of work (and you might be surprised just how much they actually care and want to see your business doing well), they will be happy to learn that a customer thinks your business is doing well. Such a bright piece of news, even if they had nothing to do to earn that particular 'wow', might cheer them up to think that 'things are not going all that badly'.

Indeed, learning of a 'wow' being earned in a different department might encourage them to try to earn one for their own department.

Sometimes we're a little diffident when we receive a 'wow'. Humility makes us reserved about how much we decide to tell other people. Well, for one, I wouldn't be shy about it – if you relate your good fortune to others in a humble manner, they will see the 'wow' for what it's really worth (and that you are not bragging for the sake of it) and they might learn from your successful actions what they have to do to win a 'wow'. They could then decide to copy you – which would be great.

But if you decide not to pass on the details of your 'wow', you can spread its good effects in another way. You can go and give a 'wow' to someone else in your business – or maybe some supplier who's done your business a good turn – and thereby keep the good effect of the 'wow' alive, rather than letting it die on your desk shortly after arrival.

62 Don't ask customers for their account number

When someone told me of this wheeze, a penny dropped. We have all got so used to having our account number handy when we phone a business that I had forgotten what life was like when we didn't need an identification number before we could talk to someone.

Without realising it, we had been getting it right in our business. But it took a client to tell me that the one reason he liked doing business with us was because we never asked telephone callers for their account number.

These numbers are like access keys. 'Oh, no, madam, if you don't have an account number, there's no way we can help you.' So when you phone a place of business and you say whom you would like to speak to and someone simply says, 'putting you through', treasure the moment and realise that it's a fast-disappearing instance of good telephone manners.

As a business owner, if this is a barrier you are putting up to callers, please find a way of taking it down – point 77 may help.

63 Don't keep your customers waiting

In a way, this point shouldn't have to be written – it's so obvious that customers should never be kept waiting. But it does need writing because *so often* we're kept waiting and sometimes for a very long time.

Take a visit to the doctor, the dentist and particularly a hospital appointment. Isn't it dreadful how often these people tend to keep us waiting? First of all, it's discourteous but secondly, it makes the doctor's surgery look inefficient. Indeed, the anguish caused by the length of the wait may even exacerbate the complaint you are suffering from.

Someone who works for me and who has just had a wisdom tooth removed, awoke at 2am screaming in pain and decided to go to the A & E department at the local hospital. Once there, he had to wait for two hours, writhing in pain all the while, only to be told at the end, 'Oh, we don't do teeth. You should go to your dentist.' Isn't that just frightful?

In our business, we try never to keep anyone waiting. It can happen, but if we have kept our clients longer than the time for their appointment, we have some antidotes. They can:

1. read our book of jokes;

2. look for the mice that Terence Cuneo has hidden in the prints we have hanging on our walls;

3. have a cup of tea, etc.;

4. make another appointment, for which we would offer to visit them by way of apology.

They will also be kept fully informed of how much longer the wait is likely to be so that they will know that the wait shouldn't be forever – or if it's going to be for a long time (the person they are due to meet has been held up in bad traffic, etc.), they then have the knowledge and flexibility to control the situation and reschedule the meeting, if they wish.

Try to make sure that waiting never happens in your business. If it does, work with your staff to find ways of ensuring it stops happening.

64 How to deal with complaints

First of all try to look on a complaint as being an opportunity rather than a problem. This is easier said than done because when a customer moans, we all tend to cringe – being human we naturally hate such moments, and it's hard to look on them positively. The reason that complaints are blessings in disguise is that if handled properly, you can often find that you end up creating a bond between yourself and the complainer that is considerably stronger than it was before the complaint was made. But the situation has to be handled properly.

First of all, try to ensure that whoever it is that receives the complaint takes ownership of the problem. Even if he had nothing to do with the problem, he should do all in his power to resolve the issue satisfactorily. Indeed, it's not a bad idea to empower everyone who works for you with sufficient authority to arrange for a box of chocolates or a bouquet of flowers to be sent to anyone that appears to have just cause for complaint.

The reason you should get everyone who works for you to own any moan that comes his way is that so often (so infuriatingly often) whenever we make a complaint, we get passed from pillar to post; each time we discuss a problem with the relevant business, we find that we never speak to the person we first raised the matter with, and always have to explain the situation again because the listener doesn't know what we're on about. Doesn't this drive you to distraction?

But it's more than getting just one person (the first who hears of it) to deal with it. Whoever it is must understand that the person complaining would not be complaining if he didn't think that he had a grievance. In other words, sympathy and understanding must be shown at every turn. We must try to get ourselves into the customer's shoes and see what it is that he sees.

If we do this, rather than put up defences, we will quickly see what the problem really is – we might even see that it's all a big misunderstanding and can put the complainer's mind at rest. But if we reply by saying things such as, 'Didn't you read what it said on the label?', 'That's not our fault', 'That's down to you' or 'We accept no liability', while you might win the battle and watch the complainer storm off, that person will foulmouth you to his friends. It could also cause a whole lot more bother and cost through lost business than if you had accepted the blame, paid up and left him amazed at how easy it was to get recompense for what he perceived as being your fault. Indeed, this is one of the beauties of having great guarantees. When someone complains, you say, 'Oh, we have a guarantee that will look after you – shall I tell you what it says?' He will become putty in your hands once he realises that there's not going to be a fight!

65 Part on good terms

This is closely aligned to the last point.

We all lose customers. They die, they move away, they find a supplier sets up in the next-door house, etc. We never keep all our customers. So when a customer leaves your premises, remember that it could be for the last time. Indeed, when you think about it, every customer will experience that moment when he walks away for the last time and often neither side will realise that it's the very last time that one will see the other.

Sometimes these last moments will be because the customer has had a raw deal (or thinks he has), but even if there's been no problem at all and neither side realises that this is the last time each party will do business together, you should make sure that he leaves you happy.

This can be achieved by being cheerful, or cracking a light-hearted joke, or asking after his health, or simply by listening patiently. It could be that you walked with him to the door or, better still, to his car.

If he leaves your premises, whether it's for the last time or not, and he's thinking happy thoughts about you, your product and your level of customer service, he will leave you as an 'ambassador' for your business. He will be in the mood to recommend you, or perhaps even defend you if he comes across someone who is attacking your reputation.

I remember making such a discovery when my firm was dealing with a case that involved both a client and that client's solicitor. Both the client and I were trying to coax the solicitor into action and the solicitor complained to our client that he could never get hold of me. Now, we can all be difficult to get hold of from time to time, for whatever reason, but I was pretty certain that, in this particular context, I had not been inadvertently playing 'hard to get'. I hadn't seen the client for some time but she phoned me up and rather than asking me why I had neither received nor returned the solicitor's phone calls, she said, 'Of all the people and of all the businesses, yours is the easiest I have come across in terms of getting through to the person I want to speak to. I know that the solicitor hasn't really been trying, he is just pretending that he had tried to contact you.'

So, here we have a case of a client appreciating the way she has been treated by us, to such an extent that she instinctively came to our defence. Now, they don't all do it, but this instance shows that it's important always to try to part on good terms. You have no idea how long the good impression will last.

66 The dangers of lowering the price

Lowering the price is the way we all instinctively feel we should go if we're to attract more customers. Indeed, when you see signs everywhere for 'sales', 'free offers', 'buy one get one free', 'never knowingly undersold', we all tend to think that lowering the price is what others do and that we have to do the same. This view seems to be confirmed when we hear our friends showing off about how little they paid for something. Paying little seems to be not just the norm, but the only way to do things. I beg to differ…

For a start, if you look at the following table, you will see exactly how much more you would have to sell if you were to lower your price by a certain percentage. If you have a gross margin (this is synonymous with gross profit, by the way) of 40 per cent and you reduce your prices by 10 per cent, you would need to sell a third more than before, just to keep even. In other words, reducing the price could well be the worst thing that you ever do.

If your present margin is...									
	20%	25%	30%	35%	40%	45%	50%	55%	60%
	To produce the same profit, you must increase your sales volume by...								
And you reduce your price by...									
2%	11	9	7	6	5	5	4	4	4
4%	25	19	15	13	11	10	9	8	7
6%	43	43	25	21	18	15	14	12	11
8%	67	47	36	30	25	22	19	17	15
10%	100	67	50	40	33	29	25	22	20
12%	150	92	67	52	43	36	32	28	25
14%	233	127	88	67	54	45	39	34	30
16%	400	178	114	84	67	55	47	41	36
18%	900	257	150	106	82	67	56	49	43
20%		400	200	133	100	80	67	57	50
25%			500	250	167	125	100	83	71
30%				600	300	200	150	120	100

At point 40, I dealt with the alternative way of looking at this (namely adding value to what you do rather than lowering price). There is, however, another aspect to this matter: if you are seen as cheaper than the rest, this actually lowers your esteem in the eyes of the buying public. But if you are the most expensive and are known to provide an excellent service, this raises your reputation.

67 It takes five calls to make a sale

Some of you may smile when you get to the next point, when I moan about the whole business of making cold calls on the phone, but this point isn't intended to contradict the next one. Instead, this point emphasises the importance of perseverance.

Just because someone said 'no' when you went to see him (or he called to see you) doesn't mean that he will always say no. We all have a habit of changing our minds.

What I have specifically in mind here is that when you have a meeting with someone who may want to buy from you but doesn't want to buy on that first occasion, you should always ask him if he would like to be on your mailing list, or to receive your regular newsletters, or to be invited to product launches. You tell him that there's no charge and no obligation, and the chances are that 50 per cent of the people you approach in this manner will be happy to say yes – they will be happy for you to keep in touch with them.

You then put these customers' details into your database and make sure that they get a mailshot each time you send one. And, in due course, you will find that gradually some of these people will come back and buy. But it could take you five such moments of contact before they want to become a customer.

The point here is that most people in the world will never buy from you. It's a given and a bit of an unwelcome given at that. But if one, or more, of these people has made some sort of approach to you (he has approached you, please note, not the other way around), he is far more likely to buy from you than someone who has never even heard of you.

So if he has paid you the compliment of enquiring about your products, that's a compliment worth treasuring and you should, indeed, value it, nurture it and use it. That person could well become a real customer in due course, but it may well take five return approaches before he does.

Are you being gently persistent with your prospective customers?

68 Don't cold call

Now, lots of people would disagree with me over this point, but I rest my case on the observation that I hate receiving cold calls. (I take it that we're agreed that cold calling means phoning complete strangers up and trying to get them to buy something?) Why do I hate them?

- Cold calls interrupt what I'm doing.

- The caller never asks if he is interrupting me and should he call back later.

- The caller is often hard to understand.

- The cold caller starts from a totally unavoidable advantage – it's very rare for anyone to leave a ringing phone unanswered – and the very fact that we picked up the phone and said hello makes it difficult for us to say to him 'get lost' politely. We resent the fact that, unwittingly, we have passively invited him to tell us what he wants us to buy.

- It's sometimes evident from the pause before the caller starts to speak that he has set about three phones ringing in the hope that someone will be at home.

If you too regard cold calls in this light, you should never inflict this sort of suffering on your potential customers.

69 Client surveys

I have touched on customer advisory boards before and if you can get them to work (by persuading customers to turn up and tell you what they think of you), they are the best way to learn how well you are doing.

The next best way is to write to your clients, asking them to spare you a few moments by writing back with their thoughts on your business. Don't expect everyone to reply, but those who do are the ones who really care.

Here is the best way to do it:

First of all, make it easy for your clients to respond. The sheet that you send out can be either posted back (i.e. Freepost) or it can be faxed back to you. You can email it if you want. This looks pretty efficient but I'm not sure it's the best way. When I want to put my thoughts down, I'd prefer to take it slowly and deliberately. Email responses have that aura of let's get this done in the least time and then we delete it and forget it. However, I may be wrong and I'm happy to be overruled on this point.

Secondly, make it easy for them to see what you are asking so that their answers are clearly related to your questions. I suggest that you ask the same questions that you might ask if you are going to hold a customer advisory board and that you leave a few lines for them to jot down their thoughts before posting/faxing it back to you – see point 93.

Send it out to as many clients as possible and do it at least once a year.

70 A template for a client survey

Here is a template you might use:

Dear_____

We are conducting a survey of our clients and we would very much value your thoughts on how you rate our product or service.

If you have the time, please answer the following questions and either post this survey back to us in the enclosed Freepost envelope or fax it to us on the number shown at the bottom. Many thanks for taking the time to do this for us.

1. What do we get right – what do you like about our service/ product?

   _____

   _____

   _____

2. What do we get wrong – what do you dislike about our service/product?

   _____

   _____

   _____

   _____

3. What are we not doing that you wish we would do (this is not quite the same as number 2)?

   _____

```
_____

_____

_____

_____
```

4. How many marks out of ten would you give us?

```
_____
```

5. What would we have to do to score higher than this?

```
_____

_____

_____
```

Signed _____

Dated _____

Your phone number (if you would like us to call you about your comments): _____

Please now either post this back to us, using the enclosed Freepost envelope, or fax it to us on 01234 567 890.

Thank you again for your time.

71 Marketing should be a specific job and not a part-time activity

There is a tendency in small businesses to give marketing activities (selling by phone, sending out regular mailings, designing advertisements, sending off press releases, etc.) to some poor soul already busy in another part of the business, which he can do in his spare time. This is a mistake and explains why so much marketing money is wasted.

Consider that, for every business, there are three main functions:

1.   Production – the product or service has to be made or supplied.

2. Marketing and sales – having made the product you have to find customers and sell your product to them.

3. Administration and finance – the whole business has to be administered, the employees paid, the windows cleaned and the money banked.

Each of these is a vital function, so why give the employee who comes in three mornings a week to write up the books the job of marketing in your company? He will have skills in book-keeping but (almost certainly) not in marketing. Marketing and sales are so important that you need employees trained in marketing.

72 A marketing letter template

Dear_____

Would you like a **free** _____, as well as one for a friend of your choice?

There are no catches in this. We are offering a number of people a free _____, whether or not you become a customer of ours. All you have to do is fill in the attached card and post it back to us, completing all the sections, and we will post you, by return, your own free _____.

If you do not wish to keep the gift, there is no need to return it. However, if you do wish to return it, we will enclose a Freepost label for you to send it back to us at no cost to yourself. But, as I say, even that you are not obliged to do.

Why are we doing this?

We are a business that started __ years ago. We believe that what we do is of very high quality and we would like to introduce you to our high standards by sending you something that is unique to our business, demonstrates the quality we always aim for and that we hope you will find to be of value.

Having done this, we hope that you will think well of us (perhaps say nice things about us and show off the _____ to your friends).

We would also like to add your details to our database so that if we decide to make further free offers in the future, we can keep you informed.

If you have a friend that you think would also like a free _____, simply give us his name and details, where applicable, before you post the card back to us.

We look forward to hearing from you.

Yours sincerely

_____

73 How to write a reply paid card

As we have seen, this can be a sheet for faxing back. In many ways, a simple A4 sheet and Freepost envelope is the easiest for both parties.

Please fill in all the boxes

To: _____

Your name: _____

Your business: _____

Your address: _____

Dear _____

Thank you for the invitation and, yes, I would indeed like a free _____. Please send it to me at:

_____

_____

_____

My other contact details are as follows:

Tel: _____

Mobile: _____

Fax: _____

Email: _____

My friend who would also like a free _____ is called:

_____

His address: _____

_____

_____

His other contact details are as follows:

Tel: _____

Mobile: _____

Fax: _____

Email: _____

I understand that we are both entitled to keep each of our _____ and that we are not obliged in any way to pay for this gift. I also understand that you will be adding our details to your database and may inform us of further offers from time to time in the future.

Signed _____

Date _____

74 One thing at a time

Rome wasn't built in a day. In other words, you won't change your business or its profits overnight. But don't be downhearted. As I hope you will have gathered, if you set your hand to the plough and start to turn things around, it will come right and probably sooner than later.

So while you need to accept that things will happen in their own good time, you simply have to start somewhere (preferably one place and not more than one) and run with that one (first) thing you have opted to do.

When that is turning over and things are starting to change, then start the next. But please don't think, 'Oh, this mountain is so steep and tall. There's no hope that things can ever get better or any different. I might just as well struggle on as I always have.' This is *not* the result I want to see from you reading this book.

So would you do me just one favour? Select just one of these ideas (or one of your very own) and, having shared it with someone, give it a go and see what happens. I hope that you will be pleasantly surprised.

75 Don't argue

Let me share with you an example of how a prominent telephone company got it wrong and why I will never do business with it again.

In April 2000, I bought a mobile phone from a firm for just under £100. It came with the guarantee of £50 cashback and a second mobile phone for my wife. The phone duly arrived by post, but no cash ever came and neither did the extra phone. I chased up enquiringly for both these items over the ensuing months but neither of them ever arrived.

After I had had the phone for a month, I discovered that, in order to use it, I had to top it up every month, even if there was a healthy credit balance on board. (I was never told this when I bought the phone.) This proved an incredible nuisance.

I used to find that when the (boring) monthly top-up time came along, it had to happen just at the time I wanted to make an urgent call, it took about ten minutes to do and it was extremely irritating because I found that the phone company could not accept my credit card details. This had nothing to do with my credit card balance – it was due to a company computer misreading the numbers I had punched into my machine. I kept checking the screen to see that I had entered the numbers correctly and each time I had, but when the automatic voice read them back, it always advised me that I had entered different numbers.

So I telephoned the helpline. This was not easy, but I won't go into that particular rigmarole. All I will say is that you would think that a telephone company would have the best telephone techniques – I have seldom encountered worse.

Anyway, by this time I was pretty fed up with the phone company and when the lady (eventually I found myself talking to a real human being) eventually answered me she said, 'We'll go through the procedure with you so that I can see what you are doing wrong.' (At this point my months of exasperation leapt into fury.)

After the call ended, I penned an angry letter to the managing director of the phone company and returned the phone to him by recorded delivery. The letter gave him full rein to make things better, had he bothered to read it. Do you think he did?

What do you think happened? Nothing. At least nothing for six weeks. Six weeks!

Eventually, at the end of October 2000, a delightful lady, by the name of Mandy Baxter, telephoned to say that the company had my letter but had lost the telephone. She was delightful because she seemed to care. She said 'Sorry' more than once. This was something her managing director didn't seem to know how to do.

In early November, Mandy said that I would be refunded the unused balance on my account. She had no authority to offer any sort of recompense; so at least I was not out of pocket.

Unfortunately, there was a further problem brewing with this case. I had thought that I had paid for the phone in April by credit card. I had received no invoice, neither had any reminders come in the post and I was sure I wouldn't have received the phone without having paid for it first. Apparently, I had not paid for it.

Unbeknown to me, this debt was placed in the hands of debt collectors who, in early November, sent me a demand for an unspecified £99.99. I replied to them asking what it was for. They didn't reply. However, I eventually twigged that it was for this unwanted and returned mobile phone. I explained this to them and they seemed to back off. But not for long.

In early December they telephoned me in a very hostile way saying that they would see me in court unless I sent them proof that the debt was not due to be paid. I was flabbergasted. The phone company had already told me four weeks earlier that the debt had been cancelled and here were their debt collectors taking me to court for the same debt. I tried to get a word in edgeways to say that the debt had been cleared, but I was denied the right to speak. I had to send proof. The debt collectors were not interested in what the phone company had to say and if I failed to pay, they would see me in court.

I did what the man angrily demanded, but not without making an additional complaint to the managing director of the phone company, sending him details of the debt collectors' appalling behaviour. At the time of writing this point, I have had no response from the phone company.

This story is included in this book to show how vital it is to remember not to cheese the customer off and especially not to argue. If I had been properly treated, I would never have included this tirade. But as it was so bad, I feel that I have to tell you to demonstrate exactly how not to look after the customer.

Essentials for the longer term

76 Newsletters

If you read the advice given to you by the great marketing gurus, you will be encouraged to communicate with your customers every month. Now, this will seem to be a bit of a chore (unless you have an employee or department whose job it is to make sure the monthly mailing happens), but it does work.

Let me give you an example:

Laithwaites, the wine-by-post people, is a very good example of what I mean (even though some will say that it probably overdoes the regularity of the mailings). Once you have bought from this company, you are likely to hear from it at least once a month. Laithwaites send out easy to use order forms, the products are first rate and you can be sure that, unlike wines you may buy in a supermarket or off-licence, it has selected the wines that it likes on the supposition that you will like them too. You can learn about the wines on offer from the promotions and the whole experience is:

1. very easy;

2. very efficient; and

3. effective – you need never be without a decent and reasonably priced bottle of wine again.

The chances are that you don't sell wine by post. However, you must sell something, so why not write about your product or service, get it nicely printed and post it to the customers on your database?

You shouldn't be overtly selling yourself or your business (customers don't tend to like it), but you should be seeking to entertain and amuse your clients (they always like jokes and cartoons, no matter who is sending either to them). If they are interested in finding out more about the product or service, you should provide them with a phone number, or a form they can fax or post (Freepost again comes in handy).

One reason why you should do this is that even when we get a wonderful service or product, most of us don't remember where we got it from; the longer time passes, the less we remember who it was that knocked us off our feet. We forget names and we certainly don't remember phone numbers (and, for all we know, your business may have changed its name or moved).

So the chances are that even though they bought from you once and think you are great, customers will not buy from you again because they don't know how. But if you send them newsletters each month and they are attractively designed and a pleasure to receive (in other words, they don't look like cheap junk mail), you will retain a far greater proportion of your business.

77 Telephone techniques

It's extraordinary how few people know about the vital importance of using proper telephone techniques. Most businesses are very bad at answering and conversing on the phone, and we all know of bad examples like these:

1. 'Hello, XYZ Company.'

2. 'How can I help you?'

3. A mumble so indistinct that you don't know whether you have heard correctly.

4. 'What's your account number?'

5. 'Hold on, I'll see if he's free.'

6. The dreaded press-button automatic switchboard answering service.

I would love to pass a law forbidding all of these.

The best way to answer the phone, whether you are a receptionist, the boss or anyone in a business, is to pick up the phone and say, 'Hello, XYZ Company. This is Tim or Jenny.' This is all the caller wants to know and it gives him a wonderful launch for him to say, 'May I speak to Mr Smith, please?' If Mr Smith isn't already speaking on the phone, you put him through.

Finally, and this will surprise you, you should *not* ask the caller for his name, unless he volunteers it to you. This sort of interrogation is very unfriendly.

If you answer the phone like this, you will find:

- that people start to say how friendly your business is;

- that Mr Smith gets very good at politely ending calls from unwanted salespeople;

- how maddening it is when you call the myriad of other businesses that blindly commit the six crimes mentioned above.

Now, Mr Smith is entitled not to receive calls if he doesn't want to. When this is the case, he tells everyone that he doesn't wish to be disturbed. Under these circumstances, when someone telephones to speak to Mr Smith, the person who answers the call says, 'I'm afraid Mr Smith isn't available. Shall I get him to call you back when he's free or maybe there's some way that I can help you?'

78 Write a quote that won't put your customers off

Most people get quotes wrong because they fall into a common trap. This trap is to put the price at the bottom of the letter. It's the last thing the reader gets to and it's often more than he was expecting, so he tends to say, 'What! I'm not having that. Let's find someone cheaper' and you don't get the business. The way to avoid this trap is to *start off* by mentioning the price. Here is an example:

Dear Mr Jones

Thank you for asking us to quote for replacing the gutters on your house. As you know, we have surveyed your present system and we believe we should replace all the present guttering.

Our price for doing this will be £1,500 + VAT.

In reaching this price we have included a number of extra benefits that we think you would find attractive and these include the following guarantees:

- We will do this at a time that suits you. If you want it done next week, we will ensure that this occurs.

- If you do not want us to arrive before a certain hour (say 9.00am), simply tell us.

- Having carried out the work, we will call back in a month's time to ensure that the new gutters are performing satisfactorily.

- We will do the same each spring for the next two years (after the winter gales) and replace any damaged guttering free of charge.

- We will provide all our own scaffolding and ladders for this work. Our equipment is so designed not to damage grass, flower beds or garden paths.

- While carrying out the work at gutter level, if we notice any problems with your tiles or other roofing materials, we will report these to you. We will be happy to repair any minor matters at no cost.

- Again, while carrying out the work, we will use our special flushing equipment to ensure that all your down pipes (which we believe do not need to be replaced) and connections to the main drains are clear.

- Finally, the materials from which our guttering is made come with a ten-year guarantee, so if any guttering proves to be defective during this time, just call us and we will replace it free of charge.

Yours sincerely

_____

If you would like us to proceed with this work, either call us on the above number or, if you prefer, post or fax the attached sheet back to us.

There now. Aren't you more impressed by the extras you are going to receive than are upset by the price? Doesn't this layout make sense?

79 Make it easy for your customers to buy from you

Having made your sales pitch and got potential clients interested, you have to keep the momentum up. If you let the matter drop and leave them to think about it, while they may seem to be very interested initially, they may not proceed because they get tied up with work and other priorities divert their attention.

Now, what I'm about to recommend is in no way 'hard selling'. It's business courtesy and good manners.

At the end of the previous point I suggested that you offered your prospective customers a 'fax-back' form or equivalent. If you do, and I think you should, this is how it might be worded…

To: [_insert the name of your own business_]

[_Insert your address or fax number here_]

_____

Thank you for your quotation.

I accept the service (or product) that you are offering and at the price you have quoted.

Please would you deliver (carry out) the product (work) on or by

_____.

I would like to pay for this work by Standing Order over [*insert number*] months. Please send me a Standing Order form.

While writing to you I have the following comments or additional requests to make:

_____

_____

Please contact me to confirm these arrangements.

Yours sincerely,

_____

Do send customers a Freepost envelope in case they want to post this sheet back to you.

80 KPIs

KPIs stands for Key Performance Indicators. These are the things you measure on a regular basis to see how well or badly your business is doing (that's their first use) and their second use is even more important – KPIs enable you to manage your business better.

So how do you recognise a KPI when you see one?

The first KPI one thinks of, although it's not that useful, is the annual profit and loss account. This shows you what your sales have been, what your direct costs have been, how much your overheads were and what profit or loss you made. So, while it's an account (in other words, it tells a story), it shows you four vital figures, as well as other detailed figures that are key to measuring the performance of your business.

But this set of KPIs isn't that useful because it's usually prepared some months after the end of your accounting year, so it can be historical. It's not much use in terms of giving you up-to-date information.

So let's look at some big, bold and better KPIs.

The first is the bank balance. You might have a sheet in which you list the daily, weekly or monthly bank balance, so that you can see how it's moving, thus keeping a close and regular watch on where it's headed.

Then there's the figure of sales. Again, this could be daily, weekly, monthly and indeed it could (and should) be broken down between the different types of sales that you make.

Then there's the number of customers you have. You list the new ones that arrive and spot those that leave you. (In spite of your best efforts, you will find that this second figure is depressingly higher than you think it is. Customers die, move away, no longer have a need of your product or service. Just because they were customers last week, this is no guarantee that someone else won't wow them more than you have and that they will be won over to a rival tomorrow. This problem is what this whole book is about – customer winning and customer retention.)

Below I list a whole range of KPIs for you to consider using. You won't need too many, but you will want to have the right ones.

Some KPIs in regular use

To make this work, you should develop a simple template (a blank sheet of paper, even), on which to record the statistics that drive your business. It can even be handwritten – whatever you find suits you best. The key is to keep the template and use it to manage your business better.

Sales related

- Sales in money
- Sales in numbers of sales
- Average sale
- Customer complaints and the percentage resolved
- Price of goods sold
- New products launched
- New guarantees launched
- New customers

- Customers lost

- New customer accounts opened

- Customer survey results

- Advertising costs

- Stocks held

Employee and productivity related

- Sales per employee

- Number of years' service of your employees

- Employee satisfaction survey results

- Absentee rate

- Hours of training by employees

- Costs of training and professional advancement

Other KPIs, yields, ratios, etc.

- Cash balances

- Money owed by your business

- Money owed to your business

- Gross margin

- Net profit percentage

- Dividends paid

And for the more technically minded

- Working capital

- Creditor and debtor turnover ratios

81 Testimonials

There are two ways to handle testimonials. There's the British way of not asking for them and, when they come, doing nothing with them except filing them. Then there's the American way, where you actually ask your customers for a testimonial and you put them all in a book which you leave in your reception (or on your website) and milk them for all they are worth. I'm not sure which is the better, but I suspect that it's somewhere between the two.

Before I carry on, you may be wondering what a testimonial is. According to the compact Oxford English Dictionary, it's a 'public tribute to someone and their achievements'. They tend to be written but occasionally form part of a verbal citation. The kind that I'm thinking of is usually written.

We British tend to be diffident about flaunting our testimonials as it's considered to be bad form to show off, but I think this view is mistaken. When something has been well done and well received I consider it a duty to make sure that the good news is shared and broadcast.

I think the best way to tackle this issue is to say to your customers: 'By the way, if what we do for you works well, do let us know. The rest of the team do like to know whether they are getting it right, so we'd be delighted to hear from you if you like our service/product. If you should say something in this respect, may we publicise it?'

(By the way, don't let on, but most clients love being asked for their views and if their opinions are going to be publicised, this makes them even more willing to help in this regard.)

And, of course, this is where a digital camera comes in handy. You can take a photograph of those who say nice things about you. Then, if you do publicise their testimonials, you will have a photograph of the customer to go with it.

82 Use a digital camera

Now, this is an idea that I have yet to use properly myself, but I can already see the sense of it for many businesses.

If you have a camera (and the flexibility that a digital camera offers makes it easily the best option), then use it in your business. Try to have it with you at all times.

You can take photographs of:

- customers using your products;

- the thousandth customer to visit you;

- employees who have passed exams, achieved qualifications, etc.;

- the lady who answers the phone, whom the customers never see;

- customers' portraits;

- before and after photographs of customers' premises (i.e. before and after you have benefited them);

- and more; I'm sure you will have plenty of good ideas.

The ease of digital photography makes converting these photographs and using and benefiting from them extraordinarily quick. This enables you to build up a supply of interesting and fun photographs to put into your monthly newsletter.

In fact, you will find a thousand and one ideas for using such a camera, but can you see how it adds to the difference you can score over your competitors who would never dream of using one and turning it to their advantage?

Quick ideas to put into practice

83 Freepost envelopes

There is a well-worn maxim, so well worn that you will find it cropping up more than once in this book, which says that 'you simply cannot make it too easy for your customers to do business with you'. If you do make it difficult, in any way, they will tend to buy from someone whom they find more convenient.

One of the best ways of helping them communicate with you is to pay for their postage. Take one obvious example: Let's say they owe you money because they buy from you on credit. So, and this applies particularly if they are private individuals, when they receive your invoice or statement through the post, they have a number of things to do before you get their money. They have to:

1. get their chequebook out;

2. write the cheque;

3. find a suitable envelope;

4. address the envelope; and

5. stick a stamp on it.

Bearing in mind that they will have had to:

6. buy a stamp in the first place; and then

7. post it.

That's at least seven activities that they will have had to undertake if you are to get your money. However, if you had supplied them with a Freepost envelope when you sent them their invoices, you would have eliminated four out of the seven activities.

This system isn't expensive (it's a service provided by the Post Office and you can set the system up by making a simple phone call to order the set-up papers) and it does make you seem more friendly to your customers than those firms that never think of offering this powerful incentive.

However, the Freepost service can be used for much more than encouraging your customers to send you money. You can use it to encourage them to:

- place their orders with you;

- complete and post survey forms; and

- make their next appointment with you.

I suspect that you will have already thought of your own particular use to which the Freepost service can be put in your business.

84 Yellow Pages

This is one form of advertising that really does work, for the simple reason that the people who use it, when looking for a supplier of a particular product or service, are actually wanting to part with their money.

Most advertising (e.g. newspaper advertisements) don't work because the readers are not interested in them; they want to read the articles, look up the football scores or do the crossword. The advertisements simply get in their way. (Classified ads are different, of course – the advertisements on those pages do tend to work, but for the very reasons I'm about to explain.)

The medium that works very well in terms of attracting new business is, of course, *Yellow Pages*. To get your *Yellow Pages* advertisement to work, you have to:

- stand out;

- offer more than your competitors; and unfortunately

- spend some money.

Below is an example of an advertisement that paid for itself within three months. During this period of time, it had brought in more business than it cost to have it included in the *Yellow Pages* for the whole year – so there must be something effective about it.

My hunch is that it:

- caught the eye (because it had a colour photograph);

- impressed people because it offered:

    1. something free (the first meeting);

    2. a guarantee (you don't pay if you don't receive value for money and you are the only judge);

    3. something convenient (easy parking); and

- mentioned a whole range of services beyond what one normally expects an accountancy practice to offer.

If you were to design something similar for your business, I suspect that it would work as well as it did for us.

85 Create a simple business plan

Most businesses don't have a plan of any sort. They remind me of that frightening maxim, 'Most people aim at nothing in life and hit it with remarkable accuracy.' In other words, most business owners never aim at creating a business of worth and, as a result, they never build it into anything of value – such businesses usually phut out and die.

So, and it's one of the key thrusts of this book, please, if you haven't already done so, write down a simple plan that pinpoints what you want to achieve in your business; something to refer to every so often of why you go to work each day.

The classic statement (and I do mean to praise it – the word 'classic' is in no way meant to imply sarcasm) runs something like this:

1. In ten years' time, I want my business to be worth £5 million.

2. To achieve this, it must make profits of at least £1.5 million.*

3. To achieve this, it must be turning over £10 million.

4. At present, it turns over £1 million.

5. So I need to increase my sales by, on average, £1 million a year.

6. This year I'm aiming to add 20 per cent to my sales figures.

7. And to do this I have the following marketing strategies:

    a. Increasing my client base by 15 per cent:

        Go on to explain what you are going to do to achieve this.

    b. Increasing the number of times my customers buy from me by 25 per cent:

        Go on to explain how you will do this.

    c. Adding 20 per cent to my prices:

    d. Etc.

(*This is because a business is usually reckoned to be worth about three times its net profit.)

Now you may need the services of an independent mentor to help you put all the bricks in place – someone to keep you honest. This is something I strongly recommend in point 7.

Of course, you can have something that is more detailed than this, but it should be capable of being boiled down to something as simple as the above seven points. To help you get started, we have repeated the seven points with blank spaces so that you can have a go yourself:

My simple business plan

1. In ten years' time, I want my business to be worth
    £ _____

2. To achieve this, it must make profits of at least
    £ _____

3. To achieve this, it must be turning over
    £ _____

4. At present, it turns over
    £ _____

5. So I need to increase my sales by, on average,
    £ _____

6. This year I am aiming to add _____ per cent to my sales figures.

7. To do this, I have the following marketing strategies:

    a. Increasing my client base by _____ per cent
        What I am going to do to achieve this:

        _____

        _____

    b. Increasing the number of times my customers buy from me by _____ per cent:
        What I am going to do to achieve this:

        _____

        _____

> c. Adding_____ per cent to my prices.
>
> Signed_____ Date_____

And then keep this in your purse or wallet – live up to it!

86 Do what you say you will or even better than you promise

This may sound unimaginative, but when you think about it, there are so many people in business who underperform.

- Builders often arrive late. They frequently take longer than they should. They may keep saying, 'I'm so sorry for the delay; I'll be with you on Tuesday' and then they could break that promise as well. All the time that they are keeping you waiting, they tend to say nothing.

- Accountants often hold on to books for too long.

- Lawyers often seem to do nothing and even that takes a long time.

- Washing machine repair people often fail to arrive at an agreed time.

- Parcel delivery people say that someone will be there tomorrow. So you take the day off and they often don't turn up.

- Doctors and hospitals give you a time for an appointment and can then keep you waiting for hours.

You will also have your own testament to this general frustration that we all come across. The above are all day-to-day experiences. Sadly, they seem to be the norm. So, if you can break this mould of discourtesy, you will get a reputation for doing what you say you will.

Now, this is difficult to do. It's so much easier to fall into the trap of being discourteous. Indeed, as we see, almost everyone does it. It's a fact of life. So you will have to steel yourself to be thoughtful if you are to be successful and you will have to ensure that all who work with you are equally determined to break the discourtesy and keep it broken.

When meeting a new customer or someone who wants a job done, one trick is to say at the start, 'I think we won't be able to start for eight weeks and then it will take three weeks once we have started' or 'there is a 21-day delivery wait on that product. But we will make an absolute commitment to have completed the task by then. If we don't (and here you bring in your guarantee) you will only pay XXX of our quotation', or 'there will be no delivery charge' or something that shows it will hurt you if you fail him. You then say, 'Is that OK with you?'

But, and the customer won't know this, you have already built sufficient contingencies into your schedule, so that you get it done well before the deadlines the customer has agreed. He will be amazed (because such service is out of the ordinary) and you can be sure he will tell his friends.

87 Work with other businesses

This is an often overlooked ploy for developing a business. If you think about it, there are a lot of other businesses that your customers do business with. You are not their only supplier.

What this means is that if you were to work with other businesses – using them for introductions to your own – you may be able to grow your customer base pretty quickly. In this way, you would help each other grow your own databases.

The word I'm after is 'reciprocity'. How might this work?

Not knowing which business you are in, let's take a classic example of two separate businesses but with (probably) similar types of customers. I'm thinking of a takeaway pizza restaurant situated near to a video shop. These two businesses could co-operate if the video shop were to take advertising space on the pizza restaurant's delivery cartons with the pizza place advertising on the video and DVD cases that the video shop hires out. Indeed, they could offer 'special deals' to each other's customers.

In your case, you might need to do some research to find out which are the businesses that serve your customers and with whom you could do a reciprocal deal. You could build up some ideas either by asking your employees if they can think of a type of business that they might want to co-operate with in this way, or by flipping through the *Yellow Pages*.

The sort of liaisons that should work are as follows:

- Estate agents with solicitors, builders, plumbers, carpet fitters, etc.

- Employment agencies with payroll bureaux.

- Printers with bookbinders, advertising agencies.

- Butchers (or any food shops) with home-delivered dinner party providers.

- Newsagents with the shop next door for home deliveries.

I hope I will have made the point, but if not, think of how much advertising costs and how much of it's wasted. If you were to share the costs of advertising (a first saving) with a business that is already dealing with people who may already be disposed to doing business with you (a second saving), it could be a worthwhile and effective allocation of your marketing budget.

88 Go in for awards

This idea may not appeal and it didn't appeal to me until I tried it. May I tell you what happened when we did?

In 2000, we saw an award for customer service being advertised in the national press and we submitted an entry. We didn't get past the preliminary stage at that time.

In 2001, the people who ran the award sent us an application form and because, by then, I was away from the office on Fridays, I had time to put together a better submission and we entered again.

We then heard that we had made it to the awards dinner and when we went to it, we were the ones invited to go up in front of the audience of 250 to receive the award.

Spurred on by this, we decided to enter for a different national award three months later (a more prestigious award) and we went and won that too.

So what, you may think? Well, yes, you may say that these awards mean nothing to either existing customers or to the outside world, but they do no harm at all and, in my view, are good for the soul. I say this because if you win an award:

- Your customers tend to say, 'well done' and they are glad to be associated with a firm that is seen to be leading the field.

- Your employees are happy to work for a firm that is seen to be a success. If you win a national award, or are even shortlisted, you are likely to appear to be better than any of your local rivals.

- You can enjoy your success by saying to your employees, 'Wasn't that good! We did it. Let's celebrate.'

Entering for awards does mean that you have to take a good hard look at what you are doing and, above all, the way you are doing it; this, in turn leads to your efforts being judged by independent experts. It's good to be checked up on in this way, especially if there's an award that you can show off at the end.

But remember…you have to be in to win it. You cannot not enter and then say, 'Oh, but we are much better than the firm that won' – even if you are – because they entered and have won the award, not you.

89 Write letters to the press

This is an interesting one and one which, like the last point, surprised me.

It's a good idea to be seen to care about local issues. It gives your firm a reputation of good citizenship. How does it work?

If there's a local issue that concerns you (and it doesn't have to be anything to do with your business or the work it does), you can be pretty certain that you will not be the only one that is bothered by it. So you should write a short succinct letter to your local press and the chances are that it will be published.

As an accountant I used to write to the press about the plight of farming in our area (I had some farming clients and they would tell me their concerns). I would find that strangers would call me up to discuss what I had said and I could tell that this gesture had gone down well. It added to our reputation.

I don't think one should be too busy at writing letters – that can make you appear to be a busybody – but sticking your head above the parapet, even though it may get shot at, has the effect of making you seem to be a leading member of the community (even if you don't think that yourself!) and it adds to the respect, reputation and standing of your business.

Having said this, I recall that, at school, I was very near the bottom of the class at English. I'm sure the masters were right to mark me down to this level but, as a result, I had no confidence in my writing ability. So it took a bit of pluck to think that what I might write could be of any interest to an editor.

But my eldest brother suggested one day that I should start writing on a particular subject and this got me going. The first letter wasn't even acknowledged but, lo and behold, a short letter I had written in response to another correspondent was published – in *The Times*, no less. This has now led to subsequent articles and, as you can see, to a number of books and now to this book.

So if a lowly English writer like me can do it, so too can you. Give it a go.

90 Work with the press

I think this is more difficult than the previous point. To work successfully with the press, you have to understand how they work and keep on submitting press releases to them, but it can all prove fruitless.

If it works, you will gain significantly from any publicity; yes, even bad publicity. The golden rules seem to be:

- Always treat the press well. Even if they treat you badly, show the other cheek and try to win them round to your point of view.

- Send in press releases that catch the eye. If you want your story to be covered, you have to be different and so 'standing out from the crowd' is essential.

We tried using the services of a PR firm. The benefit of PR firms is that they keep sending stuff to the press; they will remind you each month and will usually write the copy for you. However, even they cannot guarantee that what they submit will be published and this can be, if not expensive, poor value for money.

But a PR firm will keep you more in the public eye than if you try to do it yourself. Indeed, like marketing, it's far better to have one person doing PR than asking someone who works elsewhere in your business to do it when he has a spare moment.

If you want to do it yourself, here is a checklist for writing your own press release:

- Use your own letterhead, but include in bold lettering 'News Release'.

- Include the date you sent it in.

- State when it's meant to be released.

- Give the story a clear headline.

- Give the story in not more than 200 words (and say at the end how many words you have used).

- State where interviews can be held.

- If it's being sent in electronically, enclose a photograph.

- Give dates for photo opportunities.

- Give any background notes about what your business or organisation does and why it's different.

- Give contact numbers, even at home, for the press to call.

Press releases won't all work (and they won't all be published), but if you make it easy for the journalists, editors and newsrooms to cover your story by being helpful in this way, you will get more publicity than if you don't lay out your press releases clearly.

91 Hold seminars

This idea, like press publicity, can be a very good customer winner.

What you want to do is find a subject that will interest not just your own existing customers, but also their friends and 'the rest of the world'. Then, to make it work, you need a database of likely punters to whom you will send invitations. This can be tricky (what database can be relied upon?); the way we decided to do this was to join forces with a big business that operated in a related field and which was happy for us to add in our own expertise. (You may have spotted that this is none other than 'Work with other businesses', as we have already discussed in point 87.)

In fact, each time we did this we joined forces with not one, but two other businesses. This meant that the costs were split three ways and we had exposure to three times the number of potential customers.

In our case we decided not to charge, but don't be afraid of doing so. A price on the ticket makes it more certain that those who have said they will come actually turn up.

You should have name badges prepared for those who you know to be coming and they should be coloured. The way the colour coding works is as follows:

- Anyone coming who is an existing customer of one of the presenters should have a coloured badge. If three businesses are presenting, then there should be three differently coloured badges.

- Anyone coming who has originated from the database of people who are not already customers of one of the presenting firms should be given white badges with their names on.

The key to this coding is that you shouldn't spend too long with your own customers, but if you are talking to someone wearing a badge of one of the other two colours, you will immediately know why they are there – and in the case of anyone with a white badge, about whom you are unlikely to know anything, you can start talking to him with a completely clean sheet.

From our experience such seminars should open their doors at 4pm and begin at 4.30pm after a cup of afternoon tea. You then have three speakers talking for 20 minutes each and half an hour for questions.

You close on the dot of 6.00pm and as you close the proceedings and the punters are heading for the door, it opens before their very eyes with waiters and waitresses bearing trays of drinks and snacks. This creates a party atmosphere, your punters stay and then this is the time when you win new customers.

92 Monthly mailing

A monthly mailing takes effort, but it's worthwhile. Please accept my apologies for repeating myself but Laithwaites, the wine people, are again a great example of how to market effectively. A few years ago, I fell upon an invitation to buy wines from this firm with my monthly credit card papers. It so happened that I needed some wines, Laithwaites appeared to supply what I fancied to drink and so I placed an order. The wines duly arrived in very quick time (yes, it was an impressive service) and the wines themselves were excellent. (You can tell that I'm giving the company a customer 'wow' as I write this.)

But where Laithwaites is clever is that it didn't leave things at that. The firm obviously knew that I was someone who had bought from it in the past and, with my details on the database, sent and still send me further invitations about once a month. Most of the time the mailings go straight into the bin but, once a quarter or so, they catch my eye at a time when I need to order and I have placed various orders. It's not much – probably five cases a year.

The point of this anecdote is to explain (if the penny hasn't dropped already) that if Laithwaites hadn't put my details from my original order into its database and sent me regular mailings, the chances are that I would never have bought from it again.

Why would I not have continued to buy after my first successful purchase? Because, like most people, I would have lost the number and so it would have been more convenient for me to go down to my local off-licence or supermarket instead of ferreting about trying to get Laithwaite's details, fax number, etc.

So (and again, I'm aware that I'm repeating myself but it's an important point) even if you provide a wonderful service for someone, the chances are that while he will remember the service, he will forget who you are or how to contact you again. This means that simply being good at what you do isn't enough. Remember that you have to make it easy for your customers to buy from you and this means that you must keep in touch with them, telling them of your latest offers, new products and where you can be contacted.

I believe that the best thing to do is to send out a monthly mailing; some do it more frequently than others. Some may find this frequency irritating (which is why I think a monthly service is often enough), but I forgive Laithwaites because their products and service are so good!

93 Customer advisory boards

When we held one of these it was extremely helpful, but they can be tricky – customers may not want to come to them and they need to be held properly.

First of all, what are customer advisory boards?

They are meetings that you organise with your clients specifically to ask them what they think of you. After all, they are the most important people in your business (if you didn't have any customers, you wouldn't have a business at all) and it makes sense to ask them for their views.

What are the questions you should ask?

In principle, the meeting and discussion will find its own level, but to kick-start the process, those attending should be asked the following three questions (we've seen these questions before at point 70):

1. What does your business get right – what do they like about the service?

2. What does your business get wrong – what do they dislike about the service?

3. What are you not doing that they wish you would do (this isn't quite the same as number 2)?

If you want, you can add a fourth and fifth question:

4. How many marks out of ten would they give you?

5. What would you have to do to score higher than this?

Which customers should be invited to attend? My view is that you should ask your favourites. These are the people you want to keep serving and if you can keep them happy, they may bring their nice friends along to meet you. You can invite those you don't like (maybe the relationship is bad because you are not pleasing them) to see how you can improve your service, but be careful whom you chose as some may be critical by nature.

You should hold the meetings at a neutral venue, starting at about 11am and stopping 12.45ish, at which point you give them a buffet lunch. Ideally, you should not be present at the meeting – you arrive with the sandwiches. Instead, you should get an impartial person, possibly a client or preferably a professional consultant, to chair the meeting. This is because your customers will tell a third party what they really think. We all tend to shy away from telling those we like what our gripes are, but we loosen our tongues with third parties. But don't worry, the meeting should be recorded (an ordinary audio cassette recorder will do) and afterwards you will get to listen to what they have said. You will then learn so much you never knew and, if you take appropriate action, it will benefit your business immeasurably.

94 Different levels of service

This isn't something I have tried, but I think it could well work in a number of businesses. What does it involve?

If you were to visit my bank, as you ascend the staircase and on the first floor, you would see a sign that announces that this floor is where the privileged customers are looked after. Now, I'm a pretty easy-going chap and I'm not that bothered about whether I get first-class treatment or not, but this sign makes me wonder, 'What would I have to be to be considered worthy of being looked after on that floor?'

We all tend to want to do better, to be recognised and applauded and given the best deal. It's only human. So, in your business, could you offer a three-tier service? A gold-medal level, a silver level and a bronze or (perhaps) standard service?

If you set out to provide three levels of service and you make this plain at the outset, you are then free to describe what each level consists of and to invite your customers to join at whichever level they prefer. You'll be surprised by how many want the best.

One way you could do this would be to have a board in reception on which you list your gold-medal customers (so long as they are happy for their names to be made public in this way). You may also find other customers coming along and saying, 'What do I have to do to get onto that board?'

The point about the top level is that it probably would not cost you any more to deliver this than the lower level of service. The benefits of being a gold-medal customer are likely to be the little things that you add – the special extras that show that you care but which, in reality, are not expensive to provide; just a sign that you are trying very hard. It might be a free glossy calendar each year, the free use of your first-class lounge, the fact that they will never be kept waiting or maybe it's the fact that they will get tea served from a silver teapot. I don't know what would apply in your business but you get the idea.

It's all part of that business of us all wanting to excel. Yet some of our customers don't want excellence, they just want the job done. So why not ask your customers to choose whichever level they would like and see how many don't want the lowest. This should result in you being able to charge more and enjoy the happiness your customers exude as they realise that they are being treated by you as if they were royalty.

Slightly more time-consuming ideas for putting into practice

95 Prepare a consumer awareness guide

You may not know what a consumer awareness guide is (not many people do), but it's a very powerful tool for showing your customers how proficient you are at what you do. Most businesses prepare a brochure for their prospective clients, but few businesspeople realise that brochures tend to hit the bottom of the bin just as fast as junk mail. If I give you a brochure that aims to sell you something, you are likely to be resistant to the approach. In my view, brochures, no matter how beautifully they are prepared, tend to push customers away rather than draw them in; of course, if the customer has asked to see a brochure, that's a different matter but, on the whole, it's the other way around.

It's far better to prepare a consumer awareness guide – something for your customers to take away and find out what you do. I remember suffering from a bad back in the early 1980s. To begin with, I used orthodox medicine and the more I went the less happy I became. Indeed, I was so unsure of what they wanted to do to me that I asked the owner of the local nursing home whom she would go to if she had a back problem. Unhesitatingly, she said she would go to a chiropractor and so, having asked her advice, I took it. What happened?

Well, to start with, as I arrived and waited in reception, there were a number of leaflets explaining what a chiropractor does, so I took a few and read them later at home. (No-one in orthodox medicine had ever offered me a written explanation of what he wanted to do.) When the consultant saw me, he gave me further leaflets, this time about my particular complaint and, above all, he explained that he wouldn't do anything until he had fully investigated my problem. So I was X-rayed and went home, still in pain. A few days later, armed with the knowledge of what the chiropractor was planning to do, I went back, whereupon he showed me my X-rays, pointed out the curvature in my spine and said, 'What we are going to do is straighten it all up, as well as we can.' Now, all of this made sense in contrast to the operation the orthopaedic surgeon had been planning. It seemed just common sense and I was very happy to be treated by him.

But the key to all this is that through his leaflets (his consumer awareness guides) he informed me about this trade and what he was going to do. It was instructional and not hardselling in any way. It gave me huge confidence to know that he was sharing the knowledge of his expertise with me and wanted me to understand what was going on. In various ways, he won my confidence by giving me a number of consumer awareness guides.

Soon after this we, in our accountancy firm, prepared our own set of simple consumer awareness guides, a number of which have been published by Lawpack. Indeed, this very book is a consumer awareness guide and will form part of our firm's marketing strategy. Can you do the same for your customers? Could you write something on what you do, photocopy it and get it bound? (It needn't be long.)

96 What is your reception area like?

It's surprising how many businesses pay so little attention to their reception areas. To the owners of so many businesses, their reception areas are often places where they spend very little time, usually rushing blindly through on their way to their desks, thinking only about that first phone call they have to make, etc. To them, how their reception area looks is no more important than how the back door to their home looks.

Indeed, most business owners (myself included) are guilty of this crime. It's a case of familiarity breeding contempt. We never bother looking at our reception area or notice the impression it gives.

Yet the reception area may be the only part of your business that a visitor sees. It may be that someone breezes into your premises by accident (he is simply wanting directions to somewhere else) and all he will get is a brief impression of what your business is like. If that impression is bad (the receptionist's desk is a mess, the carpet has a hole in it, the chairs have lost their seats, the newspapers are all over the place, the windows are dirty, the place smells and there's no-one even there), he will never think of coming back when, next week, he wins the lottery and suddenly needs the first-rate product or wonderful service you supply.

I once went to the reception area of a very well-known firm of estate agents that I had never been to before, and was horrified. The reception was in a large room peopled by employees working, dashing about and talking on the phone. Someone came over to greet me and asked me to take a seat at a desk, on the other side of which a man was talking on the phone to a client. Not only could I hear every word he said (I was almost involved in the conversation), but I felt really awkward. I felt that I was intruding, that I had no right to be there.

Now, I can happily say that, as I was visiting to talk to the staff about their customer service, I drew this image to their attention and they immediately saw the need to rectify this situation. However, it took a complete stranger to notice the problem, to draw it to their management's attention and for the matter to be resolved.

It could well be that, without you realising it, your reception area gives a similarly off-putting impression.

The best way to find out is to get up, and go and have a look at it, now! Is it giving the right impression? Could it do with a lick of paint? Tell your next visitor that you are thinking of improving the reception area and ask him:

- what he thinks of it;

- what is there that he finds off-putting; and

- what needs to be improved.

97 Have easy parking

This is easier said than done for many businesses, but if you think how important it is to you when shopping or visiting the dentist to be able to park close by, you will soon twig that it's vital to try to solve this problem for your customers.

When my firm bought a practice in the centre of Plymouth the parking was so appalling that clients who had made appointments were always late. On top of this, they would arrive breathless and upset that they had had such difficulties in making their appointment.

As I have already mentioned, my company solved this problem by moving the business to the outskirts of the city where we found premises with three parking spaces right outside our front door. If I may say so, it was parking perfection. The strange thing is that businesses for so long have tended to reserve the best parking spaces for the senior managers and partners that our clients have taken quite a lot of persuading that these spaces are for them. They seem almost reluctant to use them, they are such convenient parking spaces. But, as we believe, if our customers are the most important people in any business, it's only right that they have the best parking spaces.

There is a story I must tell you about a firm of solicitors called Parnalls that I was visiting in Launceston. The meeting had gone on for longer than I had allowed when paying at the meter. I told the partner that I would have to leave the meeting for a while to repark my car and was staggered at what happened next. The partner called in his secretary and said to me, 'Tell this lady where your car is parked and she will go and place a piece of paper under the windscreen wipers telling the warden to ignore the expiry of your ticket because you are visiting Parnalls.' Off she went and sure enough, when I eventually got to my car, there was the piece of paper and I had no nasty penalty to pay.

If a firm of solicitors can get this so right, then surely it's not beyond the wit of the rest of us to make some sort of customer-friendly arrangements like this with our local car park? If you can sort out customer parking, it will do wonders for customer satisfaction.

Now it's up to you

98 Never, ever give up

You have worked very hard to get this far and you deserve a bit of light relief.

If a picture is worth a thousand words, why don't we start to close down this book with a telling cartoon? I wish I knew where this came from so I could pay fulsome praise to the draughtsperson – if you know who it was, please let the publishers or me know.

NEVER EVER GIVE UP

99 A list of suggested books to read

These are a few thoughts, but there are a great many out there.

- **Up the Organisation** by Robert Townsend

  This is my all-time favourite business book; it has long been out of print (but, as I said before, Amazon appears to have a limited supply).

- **The E Myth** by Michael Gerber

  All the truths about your business, especially the ones you don't want to be told!

- **The Small Business Handbook** by Philip and Sandra Webb

  It's a great book and comes with a very useful CD.

- **Marketing Your Services for People who Hate to Sell** by Rick Crandall

  Full of useful tips.

- **Managing the Professional Service Firm** and **True Professionalism** by David H Maister

  Full of wisdom.

- **The Way of the Leader** by Donald G Krause

  I found this very moving.

- **Exceeding Customer Expectations** by Susan and Derek Nash

  I've not used this much but it seems directed very much in the right way.

- **Managing the Customer Experience** and **Uncommon Practice**

  Both FT Prentice Hall publications – again, both just up the right street.

- **Make It Happen** by Fiona Anson

  A delightful introduction to how to get ideas under way.

- **The Seven Habits of Highly Effective People** by Stephen Covey

  A bestseller that is a must.

- **Clients Are People Too** by James Alexander

  He's a friend of mine and I love this little book.

100 It's now up to you ...

This book has not been constructed in a particularly systematic way for one very good reason. All businesses are different and there is no one way to set about growing a business. If I had started with point 1, and taken you through all the apparently logical processes that should be taken, we might have ended up with a wonderful looking map, one that is identical for both you and every other reader, but this straitjacket would have worked for very few readers, if it had worked at all.

So, rather than pretend that there is only one way to grow a business, I have splashed lots of (I hope) colourful, useful and perhaps intriguing ideas around, here, there and everywhere, so that you can think your own way through this matter. For a plan to be agreed and for it to work, you have to believe in it. You should never take a plan on my or anyone else's say-so; you must believe in it yourself and you will believe in it if you have created it yourself. Indeed, better still, if you and your team have created it, it will have a far better chance of survival and success.

So what I suggest you do, if you have not already started to do it, is go through the book again quickly and select those ideas that appeal to you and jot them down on one of the two pages (xiv and xv) at the front. If you also get your employees to do the same (let them do it their own way) and then you agree to all meet up at some neutral venue, go through all the suggestions that you have all come up with.

At the end of the meeting at which all of your collective ideas will have been discussed (and, if I haven't said this already, please stress to all who are taking part that there are no such things as silly ideas), you should have three things:

1. An action plan of top priorities that will look something like the template suggested in point 48, and which lists those things that need immediate action.

2. A second action plan of those suggestions for action once the immediate ideas have been implemented.

3. A date for the next get-together in a month or two, when you will:

   • review progress;

   • thank those who have done what they said they would; and

   • create a revised list of top and second priorities for reviewing when you meet the following time. You will then have created a process that you will use for the rest of your life in that business.

If you agree that this is a sensible idea, then it has every chance of working for you and helping you grow your business. I wish you every success.

101   The things that haven't been done before

A poem by Edgar Guest.

The things that haven't been done before,
Those are the things to try;
Columbus dreamed of an unknown shore
At the rim of the far-flung sky,
And his heart was bold and his faith was strong
As he ventured in dangers new,
And he paid no heed to the jeering throng
Or the fears of the doubting crew.

The many will follow the beaten track
With guideposts on the way.
They live and have lived for ages back
With a chart for every day.
Someone has told them it is safe to go
On the road he has travelled o'er,
And all that they ever strive to know
Are the things that were known before.

A few strike out, without a map or chart,
Where never a man has been,
From the beaten paths they draw apart
To see what no man has seen.
There are deeds they hunger alone to do;
Though battered and bruised and sore,
They blaze the path for the many, who
Do nothing not done before.

The things that haven't been done before
Are the tasks worthwhile today;
Are you one of the flock that follows, or
Are you one that shall lead the way?
Are you one of the timid souls that quail
At the jeers of a doubting crew,
Or dare you, whether you win or fail,
Strike out for a goal that is new?

Index

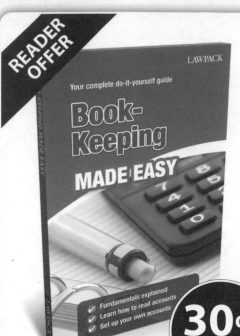